HOW TO CREATE A
WATER
CRISIS

FRANK WELSH
FOREWORD BY STEWART L. UDALL

Johnson Books: Boulder

To my wee Irish mother,
who never questioned my questioning

Cover Design by Joseph Daniel

ISBN 0-933472-88-9 (cloth), 0-933472-87-0 (paper)
LCCCN 84-063056

Printed in the United States of America by
Johnson Publishing Company
1880 South 57th Court
Boulder, Colorado   80301

Contents

Foreword

Much of the conflict over water in the West stems from the clash between two competing legal systems. By state law in most western states, surface water belongs to the first person who diverts it from the stream and puts it to a beneficial use. Thus, the farmers in the valley that is now Phoenix, by appropriating water, came to own the water derived from a vast watershed of upstream land from which the water comes.

But much of the land where the water originates is either owned by the federal government or held in trust by the federal government for Native American peoples. Here a competing federal law prevails, which, in general terms, is based on the premise that when the federal government reserved certain lands for itself, or for Indian tribes, it reserved water rights which were suitable to the purposes for which the land was withdrawn. For example, if the federal government set aside land for an Indian reservation, it by implication reserved the rights to as much water as might be needed by the Indians for such uses as drinking and irrigating crops. Thus, under one legal theory, the water was owned by downstream users, but under a concomitant principle all, or some, of it might be owned by upstream landowners. From such legal systems, intense political conflicts are born.

These legal rules are, of course, subject to higher laws, such as the law of nature—that water runs downhill. Modern man, of course, does not always abide by this law. Along with asserting ownership of water, various political interest groups may build a water project and use electricity to pump large quantities of water uphill. There is, for example, a saying in the 1980s that water runs uphill to money!

Until recently, little attention has been given in our legal system to the value of water left flowing undisturbed in a natural stream bed. Yet all recognize the beauty of natural streams and rivers. In the arid west, natural streams often have an added beauty because they support lush strips of forest which contrast sharply with adjoining deserts. In such riparian habitats, birds and mammals abound. If dams are constructed upstream, they may stop the flow of water and destroy this riparian habitat. To preserve what is left of such rich natural areas, bird watchers and conservationists often unite to battle new dams and their associated canals and pumping plants.

Another conflict exists between urban users of water and the older agricultural users. As urban growth continues, areas that were previously used for irrigated agriculture become converted to homes and industries. The urban users can afford to pay much higher prices for water than the agricultural users can afford. If there were a free market system functioning, water would be sold by the less economically productive users to the more economically productive users. While this occurs to some extent, the old concepts that water rights are tied to the land do not change easily. In fact many restrictions on the sale of water can still be found in western water law. But the clear trend in the 1980s is for the transfer of water from agricultural to urban uses to continue.

If irrigated agriculture is to remain an important component of the economic and social structure of our western states, it is vital that both urban and agricultural users increase their efforts to conserve and reuse water. Serious and substantial conservation of water will not be achieved by serving water in restaurants only when requested or by putting bricks in toilet tanks. Significant conservation of water *can* be achieved by utilizing drought-tolerant plants for urban landscaping and by innovative irrigation techniques including the laser leveling of agricultural fields and the use of sophisticated drip irrigation systems. This is now being done by innovative farmers in Arizona.

These struggles between competing interests quite often creates the impression that the western states lack adequate supplies of water. In one sense there is a shortage of water. It is true that there are vast areas of the west that could be utilized for irrigated agriculture if more water were available. There are also many areas in the west where ground water is being pumped out faster than it is replaced by nature. One important issue addressed in this book is whether the apparent lack of adequate water is a real problem or one created by our legal system.

The ultimate strength of America resides in its people. The job of governing our complex technological society ultimately rests with leaders chosen by American voters. Yet some problems seem so complex as to be beyond the grasp of the common man. In trying to understand complex issues, we must turn to independent professionals for their insights and judgment. The true professional does not seek to confuse the issues with jargon or technical details that are understandable to only a select few—but rather to set forth the issues, the facts, and his or her judgments in a way that can be easily understood by all who are seriously interested in solutions.

Recent history teaches us that our nation can take command over complex problems and work toward solutions that benefit not only this country but all mankind. *Silent Spring*, by Rachel Carson, was a book that made the complex problems of pesticides in our environment understandable to everyone. It helped to bring about a series of changes in our country and in the world through which we have begun to control the adverse effects of toxic materials on people and on the biosphere in which we live.

In this book, *How To Create A Water Crisis*, Frank Welsh takes another complex subject and produces clarity which should make the real issues understandable. But just as importantly, this author, who is trained in both engineering and law, has written a work which is technically insightful and will appeal as much to professionals in this field as it will to the general reader. Like John Gofman's monumental work, *Radiation And Human Health*, this book is a synthesis and analysis of a subject written by a man who is intimately familiar with the intricacies of the problem.

The concepts presented in this book are certain to be controversial. The author is not afraid of stepping on toes. Yet most of those who will probably scream the loudest, particularly those of the industrial, development, and agricultural groups that support new federal water projects, usually claim to embrace the free enterprise philosophy the author espouses. Frank Welsh adheres to the principles of free enterprise that made this country strong. While a major focus of this book is the subject of how our current laws have distorted competition and free enterprise, Frank Welsh is also sensitive to social and environmental issues, as his exposition concerning Native American water rights and endangered species issues amply illustrates.

Two decades have passed since my first book, *The Quiet Crisis*, was published. I then predicted that many regions of our nation would confront a "water crisis in a matter of decades." As Dr. Welsh points out in this book, many knowledgeable people believe that that crisis has arrived, but unfortunately, few people understand its complexities. In this book he uses arid Arizona to explain the crisis. He then expands his discussion from my home state to other areas of our nation. His analysis of water and federal water projects should reach a national audience. The central theme is that the water crisis has been created more by man than by nature. Welsh's recommendations center around changes in our policies, laws, and other man-made institutions rather than on costly new construction projects.

While Dr. Welsh severely criticizes many of our present agricultural policies, particularly regarding subsidies, he does make a strong defense of the small farmer. I share this concern and believe that it is important to work cooperatively in conservation efforts, not only to avoid the necessity for expending large sums on new water projects, but also to preserve farming as a way of life in the West. I have always appreciated the Jeffersonian philosphy that "the small landholders are the chosen people of God. . . ." As President Kennedy wrote in the introduction to *The Quiet Crisis*: "The Jeffersonian faith in the independent farmer laid the foundation for American democracy."

Much of Frank Welsh's experience in the controversies relating to the water crisis comes from his involvement in the political fight against Orme Dam. This proposed dam, part of the Central Arizona Project, was to be located at the confluence of the Salt and Verde Rivers northwest of Phoenix. It was opposed by a broad coalition of groups. Some were primarily interested in the rights of the Yavapai Indian community, which would have lost most of its reservation had the dam been built. Others were primarily concerned with preserving the rich riparian habitat of the area which supports a wide range of wildlife, including a rare and endangered population of desert-nesting Bald Eagles. Welsh's leadership in this coalition began because of his engineering and economic concerns, but he also developed an understanding of the stakes Native Americans have in western water issues. His chapter on Native Americans presents a side of the Indian "conquest" unfamiliar to most Americans. No bullets were fired in this encounter. For some tribes, the upstream diversion of their water supply was enough to impoverish these native farmers.

Frank Welsh not only addresses the issues related to competition for "too little" water but also discusses the problems of "too much" water. His experience with flood control problems extends back more than twenty years to a time when he worked for the U.S. Army Corps of Engineers. One of the major functions of the proposed Orme Dam was flood control, and this continues to be an area of controversy as proposed alternatives to Orme Dam are evaluated.

Frank reminds me of an Irish leprechaun. The end of his rainbow lies in the deserts of the southwest. His love for the people and natural environment of Arizona—a state he adopted more than twenty years ago—shines through in this book. The book should be of interest to everyone in the southwest, but it is more than that. This is a book that every American should read.

If you are concerned about how your tax money is being spent, you need to know the facts which surround the water crisis. If you are a conservationist, this book will increase your understanding of the impacts water projects have on our natural environment—and perhaps enable you to be more effective in preserving the beauty of our country. If you are a concerned human being, you should be aware of the threat some water projects pose to various Indian tribes.

Stewart L. Udall
Former Secretary of the Interior
November 1984

Preface

Everyone knows that water is essential to human existence, but we seldom think about it unless it stops coming
out of the faucet. Yet water is intertwined with a myriad of
issues, ranging from agriculture, drought, and energy to the
environment, floods, and sociology.

Like so many areas in today's society, water has become
a complex web of legal decisions, technical concepts, and
political compromises. This has led to what many refer to
as the "water crisis." The purpose of this book is to unravel
that web in a manner that can be readily understood by
the average American. To that end, I may have been guilty
of some oversimplification, at the expense of extreme technical accuracy, but the concepts presented are much more
important than the minute details.

Many books have been published in the last few years
on water pollution, and most Americans are now aware of
that problem. As a result, the nation is well on its way to
dealing with pollution. The water crisis goes well beyond
that issue and is the subject of this book. The massive array
of issues involved could overwhelm the reader, so each is
discussed separately. Accordingly, each chapter is relatively
complete within itself, while still being intertwined with the
preceding chapters and those that follow. While the facts
within each chapter will surprise many readers, the whole
is greater than the sum of the parts, and the overall picture
presents an alarming insight into the way America works
today.

Of necessity, the first issue discussed is whether there is
enough water for people. After crossing this threshold, the

book concentrates on the cause of the water crisis and current proposals to circumvent it. The latter are found to treat the symptoms of the crisis, rather than its cause. Other proposals are therefore presented which could alleviate and possibly stem the crisis.

No one proposal is likely to provide a cure-all to this complex crisis, however. The suggestions unveiled concentrate on approaches that involve the least involvement by the federal government and the smallest expenditure of taxpayer dollars. Market place solutions are sought where practicable. The author believes this, the "American way," could avert the predicted water crisis with the least disruption to the lives of Americans and to their environment.

This is amply demonstrated in the latter part of the book where the individual issues are applied to a single water project. The sociological and aesthetic implications of innundating an Indian tribe and endangered Bald Eagles, for example, are bound to stir controversy. Yet one need not undertake massive philosophical soul-searching after becoming aware of the issues discussed in the first part of the book and applying them to one of the nation's most controversial water projects.

Once the facts in this book are understood, it should be obvious that common sense and the free enterprise system will go a long way toward rectifying the many abuses of our water resources.

Acknowledgements

This book is the result of more than ten years of involvement with water issues. Numerous individuals participated in this effort to educate the public. Paramount among them were the original handful of plucky souls who incorporated Citizens Concerned About the Project (CCAP) in the days when it was considered heresy to even question anything the "water establishment" proposed. Their concern about fiscal and social issues overrode the predictable castigation which followed. These taxpayers added legitimacy to the outcry of those equally plucky souls who were concerned about the environmental consequences of America's water policy.

The involvement of some individuals was above and beyond the call of duty, and they must be singled out for their assistance in writing this book. Principal among these benefactors is Dr. Robert A. Witzeman of the Maricopa Audubon Society. Another is Carolina Butler, founder of the Committee to Save Fort McDowell. Yet another is Gil Venable, attorney for both Maricopa Audubon and CCAP.

It is hoped that the illustrations in this book will make it more attractive to and understandable by the average American. Credit for the original artwork must be given to Brian Evans, and Dave Campbell, who is also Chairman of the Board of CCAP.

The author is extremely appreciative of the kind comments by Stewart L. Udall in the book's foreword. For many years he has been an active leader in western water issues, as well as in a variety of conservation and Indian causes.

FRANK WELSH

I. WATER, WATER EVERYWHERE

1. The Water Crisis

"The United States of America, the richest and most powerful nation in the world, is running out of its most indispensible commodity. That commodity is clear, usable water . . ." Texas Congressman Jim Wright made this prediction as far back as 1966 in his book, *The Coming Water Famine*. In an April 1982 editorial *The Wall Street Journal* referred to water as "The Issue of the '80s." That same month the *Kansas City Times* received the Pulitzer Prize for a series on America's water resources entitled "The Next American Crisis."

Weekly news magazines ran major stories on water. According to a special report in *U.S. News and World Report*, "Farmers, cities, states, business—everyone is scrambling for shrinking supplies. The stakes are high, and the outcome will shape the U.S. for the next century and beyond." When President Reagan took office in 1981, Secretary of the Interior James Watt stated: "The biggest crisis we will face in the years ahead is water." Few doubt these predictions. Indeed, the cry has gone out that water will be to the 1980s what energy was to the 1970s.

Undoubtedly, the water crisis is real—but what is the *real* water crisis? The assumption behind all the dire predictions is that the West has reached the limits set by nature and is running out of water. The obvious solution, it seems, is to get more water—from any place and at any cost necessary. The scale of this solution is enormous. According to a General Accounting Office report, the Army Corps of Engineers and the Bureau of Reclamation had, as of October 1981, 934 authorized water projects needing about $60 billion for completion. Perhaps not an excessive price to save cities from drying up into monstrous desert ghost towns.

But if the choice is this simple—between slow death from lack of water and the application of government expertise and tax money—why is the water crisis so controversial?

President Carter created an uproar in Congress in 1977 by withholding funding for many water projects. He was supported by Howard Jarvis, national chairman of the American Tax Reduction Movement and author of California's tax-cutting Proposition 13, who called these water projects "pork barrel" and "giant boondoggles," and water and tax wasters. Most Americans backed the president, but Congress prevailed and Carter backed down.

California suffered severe droughts in the late 1970s but in 1982 voted down a $5 billion water project that was touted as essential to the people of the arid southern part of the state.

When President Reagan's budget-cutting actually resulted in increased funding for water projects, taxpayers complained that the billions of dollars spent on them annually did not help the "truly needy."

Even the suggestion that the real water crisis lies in the mismanagement of our existing resources rather than in an actual shortage needs to be explored because so much is at stake. If politicians and bureaucrats are spending billions of dollars of tax money, allegedly to solve the water crisis but in fact creating it, the issues become of concern to every citizen.

But how to sort out the myths from the facts? Many volumes on water have been written by scientists, lawyers, and engineers. These technical treatises are usually so complex that they sit on the bookshelves of the few who are paid to prepare them or implement their recommendations. Even politicians and government agencies are overwhelmed by the reams of technical data. It has reached the point where experts must be hired to explain the findings of other experts.

Concentrating on a specific case that involves most aspects of the water crisis should clarify the whole complex issue. The Southwest has the greatest natural water defi-

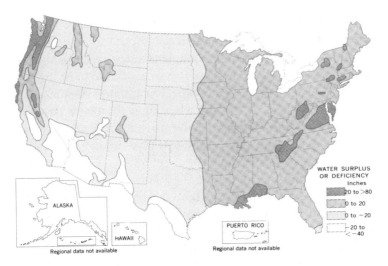

Fig. 1 Areas of natural water surplus and natural deficiency. *U.S. Water Resources Council.*

ciency of any region in the nation, and most Americans perceive Arizona as the most arid state, its cactus-studded desert seemingly crying out for water. Arizona is also one of the fastest growing states, and proponents of water projects claim that it will run out of water in the near future.

As a result, the federal government is building a massive project to transport water more than 300 miles from the Colorado River to Phoenix and Tucson—roughly the distance from Boston to Baltimore. This is the nation's most expensive water project, with an estimated 1983 capital cost of $3.5 billion. Most of the money for this Central Arizona Project (CAP) will come from the pockets of all the taxpayers in America.

Most of the water to supply the project will come from resources that southern California has been using. The rest will be supplied from water flowing in the rivers and streams of Colorado, Utah, Wyoming, and New Mexico. These states have their own water and energy projects which place demands on these same supplies and on the U.S. taxpayer. The plains states have problems similar to Arizona's and are planning their own water projects. (It has been suggested that the ultimate solution to all of these problems is to bring water from Alaska—at a cost of well over $200 billion. This would impact more than 30 states, not to mention the nation's treasury and environment.)

The CAP will consume tremendous amounts of that other precious resource, energy, as it pumps water uphill more than four times the height of the Washington Monument. This massive project encompasses virtually every issue in the water crisis, including the inundation of an Indian reservation and the habitat of endangered species, water conservation, and pollution.

But before we examine the CAP in detail we should first take a look at Arizona and see what its water crisis is all about. The "impending" crisis is upon us, so we had best take the fastest method of transportation possible. Join me on a flight across the arid Arizona landscape to the metropolis of Phoenix.

2. A Desert Oasis

Flying towards Phoenix from the east, one notices that the view below is drab and lifeless. Yellowish or reddish brown is the dominant color, and one must look hard to find a spot of green. Even the mountains are mostly bare of vegetation, appearing more as a moonscape than a landscape. Indeed, the monotonous aridity that oppresses much of the state and the searing 110 degree temperatures prompted early commentators to observe that Arizona is just like hell—both lack water and good society.

Today, though, almost three million people live in this inhospitable land, so there must be more here than meets the eye. Ironically, much of the attraction for newcomers and residents is the climate: the withering summer gives way to a warm and salutary winter, and the arid terrain gives evidence that few days are marred by clouds and rain. But this lack of moisture causes many to wonder how much longer the state can increase its population by more than 50% a decade as it did between 1970 and 1980. Where does the water to support such growing numbers of people come from?

One answer to this question is revealed as we approach our destination. Lakes appear below us, followed by a ribbon of green. These are the Salt River reservoirs, and the river flowing out of them has produced a continuous stretch of vegetation along its banks. The lake shores are devoid of vegetation, but the water is covered with speedboats, giving credence to the statement that Arizona has more boats per capita than any other state in the Union.

Downstream from the lakes, the Salt River is joined by

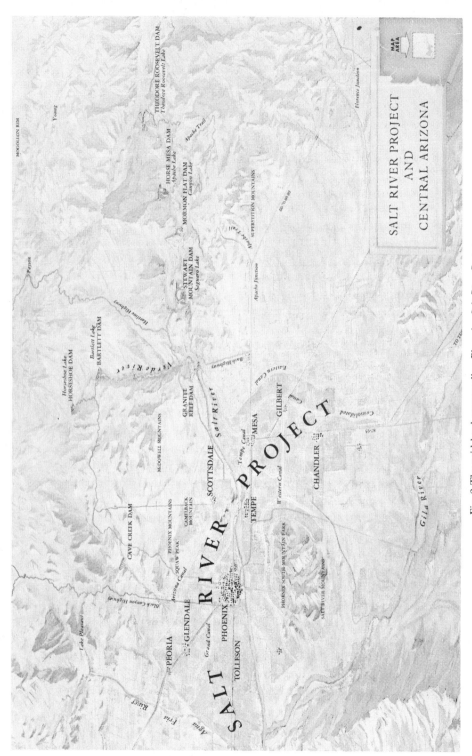

Fig. 2 The arid land surrounding Phoenix. *Salt River Project.*

another ribbon of green—the Verde River flowing from the north. A short distance below the confluence, the riverside greenery ends abruptly and the dry river bed almost blends with the dusty desert. Two thin blue lines appear at this point, paralleling the river bed. These are irrigation canals, which miraculously transform the area between them into a patchwork of green fields.

Ahead, the land is flat and almost totally developed, with a few red rock mountains emerging from the valley floor, seemingly copied by the high-rise buildings at the center of Phoenix. Subdivisions intermingle with farmlands. Each home has its own spot of blue—the swimming pool. We are now on the outskirts of the "Valley of the Sun," an oasis amid hundreds of square miles of desert. The rivers, lakes, and canals that surround it are its lifeline, without which it would presumably wither and die.

A ribbon of white is visible just beyond the northern edge of the valley. This is the Central Arizona Project canal, which would bring water to the valley from the Colorado River, more than 100 miles to the west. Some maintain that it is unnecessary, expensive and an energy waster. Others have claimed for decades that it is a much-needed, second lifeline to the valley and without its additional water the rapidly-growing central Arizona area will shrivel up.

As our plane approaches the airport, it follows the dry Salt River bed into the heart of downtown Phoenix. It is hard to believe that this river was a raging torrent in 1978 and again in 1980. Even the end of the runway was washed away. While there are those who claim it is necessary to build more dams upstream to control these floods, others say the airport and other structures which were damaged should not have been built within the river's flood plain.

The plane lands and we trade wings for wheels. As we drive out of the airport, the lush green lawns make it hard to believe that we are in a desert, but the heat assures us that we are truly in Phoenix. The radio announcer informs us that the city has had no rain for three months. As the 115-degree heat draws the moisture right out of one's body, both newcomers and natives express concern about the drought. It is an unnecessary worry, which stems from one

of the many myths about water which must be exploded—
that Phoenix itself must have rain.

In most areas of the nation such a drought *would* cause
serious problems, since the water supplies of most other
cities depend on rain falling on or near the urban area.
Phoenix is a desert city and almost by definition cannot
depend on local rainfall. It depends upon its nearby lakes,

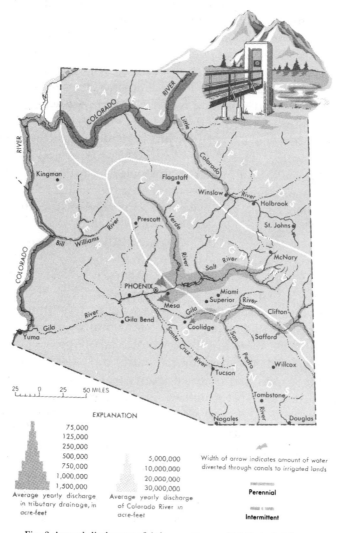

Fig. 3 Annual discharges of Arizona streams. *U.S Geological Survey.*

rivers, and canals. But where does the water to fill these originate?

Clearly the parched surrounding land could not have produced enough water to fill the huge reservoirs we saw from the air. Instead, they are fed by the rain and snow that falls on the mountains a hundred miles to the northeast. There we find the largest contiguous stand of ponderosa pine in our nation. Hundreds of square miles of this mountain belt receive as much moisture as Chicago and many areas of the East Coast.

Few Arizonans live in this moist area, because people come to the state for sunshine and cloudless skies at the lower elevations. Fortunately, Mother Nature delivers the water from the moist mountains to the desert dwellers of the Phoenix area by gravity flow—right down the rivers—without the expenditure of a single tax dollar or kilowatt of energy. It is something of a Camelot world: sunshine here, with water brought from the rain and melting snow in the highlands. This source provides the Phoenix area with a water supply which is renewed each year. But how much water does this system actually supply, and more importantly, how many people can it support?

3. Water for Cities

The myth that without more water central Arizona will eventually dry up into a giant dust bowl has been promulgated by politicians and the news media ever since Arizona became a state in 1912. It reached its heyday in the 1940s when Arizona and California were feuding over ownership of the water in the Colorado River. Figure 4 is from that era. Small wonder that most Arizonans have believed the myth!

After the completion of a state water plan by the Arizona Water Commission in 1975, headlines proclaimed that Central Arizona was facing a water crisis. The area contains three quarters of the state's population, including its largest city, Phoenix. Quoting the study, the press reported that central Arizona's renewable water supplies could support only 3.7 million people. The state's official population projector, the Department of Economic Security, estimated that 5.5 million people would live in the area by the year 2020.

But back in June 1971 Arizona's Department of Planning and Economic Development had released a report which stated:

... if all of Arizona's current water utilization was allocated to municipal and industrial use, it could support a total state population of approximately 20,000,000 persons or about one-tenth of the population of the United States in 1970.

And in 1979 the alarmist claims were countered by Herman Kahn's internationally renowned Hudson Institute. Its voluminous study, entitled *Arizona Tomorrow*, stated:

If all agricultural water was reallocated to municipal uses in 1970, the state could have supported a population of over 25 million people. . . . Moreover, this scenario does not incorporate the development of new water supplies from the Central Arizona Project or others coming on line after 1970.

There's No Arguing with Cold Facts—And Death

Without Water, Arizona's Economy Will Perish. You Have a Stake in the Fight for Water.

♦ ♦ ♦

Fig. 4 Historical cartoon. *Gaylord Pierce.*

This means that Arizona could support a population greater than that of California, the most populous state, which had 23.5 million people in 1980.

Herman Kahn's study received much publicity, and in 1981 he was selected as the Goldwater Professor of American Institutions at Arizona State University. His statements on water were generally ignored by policy makers, however.

This most important question regarding Arizona's water is also the most confusing: How great a population will Arizona's water resources support? Kahn's figure of 25 million people is based on the premise that the water now being used for irrigation has been transferred to urban use. This issue of agricultural water will be taken up in a later chapter.

An objective look at the facts will indicate that Arizona can support a much larger population than is commonly thought. (The supporting data for the following discussion can be found in the appendix.)

The Arizona Water Commission's 1975 report, which notes that central Arizona can support only 3.7 million people on its existing dependable water supply, adds that this is at the high "historic" rate of water use. It further states that with a "reasonable rate of withdrawal in central Arizona" of 200 gallons per person per day (gpd), the available renewable supply will support 5.6 million people. This takes us beyond the population projections for the year 2020.

Human beings need less than one gallon of water a day to maintain the body. Modern conveniences, however, require many times that—for example, washing machines use 30 gallons and a five-minute shower, 25 gallons.

The Arizona Water Commission's 1975 report indicates that the average water use in Arizona communities ranges from 55 to 500 gallons per person per day (gpd). Phoenix used 300 gpd in 1980; in a subsequent water conservation brochure, the city indicated that this was double the national average. Tucson used more than 200 gpd in 1974 but reduced this to 140 gpd by 1978 through an extensive public information program called "Beat the Peak." This was a voluntary program and affected only outdoor water use, primarily for watering. University of Arizona economist William E. Martin notes in his 1984 book, *Saving Water in a Desert City*, that "it would be reasonably easy to achieve a per capita use of 130 gallons per day."

There seems to be no reason other cities in Arizona cannot achieve comparable rates. In fact Arizona's 1980 Groundwater Law mandates reductions in water use by all entities. At Tucson's rate of 140 gpd, central Arizona could support more than 9.5 million people on its existing renewable water supply—a figure far in excess of the 8.6 million projected for the *entire state* by the year 2035.

For those futurists who inevitably ask "What happens then?" many paths are open. They range from the exotic to the mundane: from towing icebergs from the Arctic, to the re-use of our existing supplies. The most obvious and probably the least expensive step would be further conservation. Several Arizona communities today use water at a rate of less than 100 gallons per day, and space age technology has provided a system which uses less then one gpd. At the 100 gallon rate, central Arizona can support more than 13 million people.

Our analysis shows that Arizona has plenty of water for its citizens. Is this also true for the other arid states?

A September 1981 Rocky Mountain poll showed that nearly 60% of westerners believed that their states will face serious water shortages within 10 years. But the federal government's 1975 report, "Critical Water Problems Facing the Eleven Western States," presents a far different picture in its compilation of the renewable water supplies available to each state. The collective author of that report, the U.S. Department of Interior's Bureau of Reclamation, concurred with the Arizona Water Commission's projection that the rate of water use by Arizona's cities would decrease to 150 gpd by the year 2034. Surely other cities in the arid west can meet this criterion. Applying the 150 gpd rate to the available supplies of other states, we arrive at the supportable populations shown in the following table:

Table 1: Supportable populations with existing surface water supplies

State	Supportable Population	1980 Population
Arizona	19,700,000	2,719,225
New Mexico	13,300,000	1,295,474
Nevada	27,100,000	800,312
Colorado	39,800,000	2,882,061
Wyoming	39,200,000	468,954
Utah	38,200,000	1,459,010
California	296,600,000	23,545,061

It is surprising to find that these, our most arid states, can support populations many times greater than presently exist. But probably the most shocking figure in this list is that of California. The state has enough renewable water to support the population of the entire United States!

Yet we keep hearing about water shortages and water problems. California is attempting to build more multi-billion dollar projects to bring more water from its moist northern areas to its arid southern regions, even though the supply already available to the south is adequate to support the entire population of that most populous state!

If we look at the Denver and Salt Lake City areas, we see that they are similar to Phoenix in that their renewable supplies are limited by the amount of rain and snow falling on their nearby mountain ranges. But both communities receive sufficient water from these sources to support more than 10 million people, many times their present populations.

But another great source of water lies under these thirsty areas—groundwater. This resource and the misunderstandings and propaganda it has been subject to are the topics of the next chapter.

4. Water in the Ground

Surface water is renewed every year by rain and snow. But in addition to this resource, vast quantities of water are stored under the Valley of the Sun. It has accumulated over hundreds or even thousands of years. The Phoenix area has not only adequate surface water but also sufficient groundwater to insure itself against future droughts.

This resource is immense, and a portion of it is continuously renewed through "recharge" as surface supplies seep

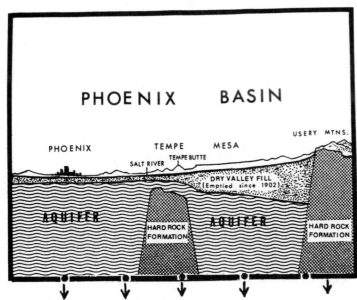

Fig. 5 Groundwater resource beneath the Phoenix area. *Brian Evans and U.S. Geological Survey.*

into the soil. Removal of this water in excess of the recharge rate is generally referred to as "mining" the groundwater.

The common allegation that the Phoenix area is in trouble because it is mining its groundwater at 30 times the recharge rate is misleading. Enough groundwater lies beneath the

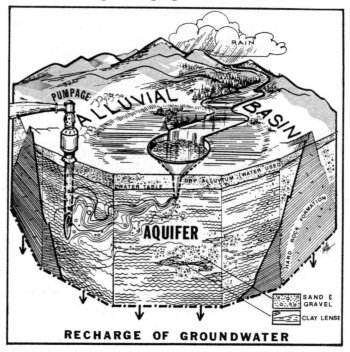

Fig. 6 Groundwater recharge in central Arizona. *Brian Evans and U.S. Geological Survey.*

Phoenix area to a depth of 700 feet to support its 2000 A.D. population for several centuries. This gives the Phoenix metropolitan area a water supply that most areas of our nation would envy. But few Arizonans are aware of its size since it is not visible. Actually, it is not known where the bottom of these underground "lakes" is, although the amounts in storage to a depth of 1200 feet are known. The experts are certain that there is additional water to depths of thousands of feet since it has been found in conjunction with geothermal and oil exploration. The known quantity of groundwater in storage under Arizona is equivalent to several times the total storage capacity of all the large reservoirs in the nation.

Tucson, like some other relatively large cities, depends entirely upon water pumped from beneath the surface, but the idea that it will dry up and blow away as a result is a myth. Though refuted by Mayor Murphy of Tucson in testimony before the U.S. Congress in 1978, this myth still persists in the Arizona news media. A more technical rebuttal was provided by the respected engineering firm of Black and Veatch. In a 1977 analysis of Tucson's water system, they stated:

The Tucson Water Utility has considerable water resources available to meet its future needs. Immediate requirements are restricted primarily by the ability to pump and transmit water from the source of supply to the point of use.

According to the Black and Veatch reports the recoverable underground supply would last for more than 230 years at the maximum projected needs for the year 2000 A.D.. That projection covers only the Tucson Basin portion of the Santa Cruz Valley. The report adds that the Avra Valley supply would be adequate for another 180 years. Additional supplies are available in the Altar Valley.

The report projects a 550-year supply for the entire area. It also states that the estimates do not include wastewater reuse, CAP supplies, or groundwater recharge. In a typical engineering understatement, the consultants added: "Conclusions reached upon our studies to date indicate quite adequate water supplies."

This study was commissioned by the largest bank in Arizona. In spite of this and other equally credible studies, the "dry up and blow away" myth persists.

At least for now, Tucson need not even mine its stored groundwater. Each year rain and snow fall on the mountains surrounding the city. Instead of being stored in surface reservoirs, the runoff from these mountains "recharges" the vast underground reservoirs, and according to the 1974 Tucson Staff Report on the CAP, this renewable supply is enough to support the city's present population well beyond the turn of the century. So neither mining per se nor the amount of available underground water appears to pose a problem for Tucson's water needs in the foreseeable future.

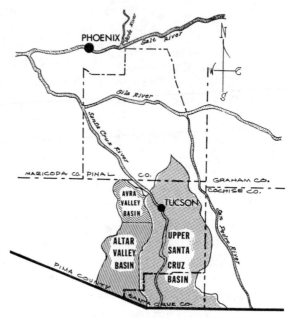

Fig. 7 Groundwater basins in the Tucson area. *Brian Evans.*

The real problem is that in 1980 the state legislature passed a new groundwater code that prohibits groundwater mining after the year 2025. The primary reason for this was to get continued federal funding for the Central Arizona Project. The water stored under central Arizona is valued on the basis of the cost of CAP water at more than $50 billion. This is surely significant in a state where the 1980 budget was less than $2 billion. University of Arizona economist William E. Martin believes that "it can be argued that leaving the same amount of water in the aquifer forever is like leaving money in a bank forever without collecting interest. Neither action produces any benefit."

Paradoxically, therefore, the law which prevents the use of billions of dollars worth of available water resources and thus "necessitates" recourse to federal funding to provide an alternative source, will ultimately, and unnecessarily, cost the state and national taxpayers billions of dollars! So, the Tucson area will indeed "need" more water in the future—even though it sits atop a tremendous underground reservoir.

Fig. 8 Groundwater recharge in the Tucson area. *Brian Evans and U.S. Geological Survey.*

Like Tucson, Salt Lake City is trying to get the federal government to construct a major water project, under the guise of needing water for municipal and industrial (M&I) use. In a 1982 article by University of Utah economists, the authors noted that in 1979 the manager of the Salt Lake County Water Conservancy District

... was quoted in the *Salt Lake Tribune* as saying, ... we are running out of (M&I) water. ... Explicit in the statement was a call for the Central Utah Project as a long term solution to water "shortages." In fact, similar expressions are frequently reported in local news media, ... However, in a March 19, 1980, *Salt Lake Tribune* article, Ted Arnow, District Chief of the Water Resources Division of the U.S. Geological Survey, was quoted as saying ... there is an enormous "overflowing" reservoir of under-

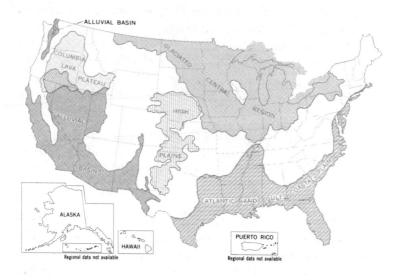

Fig. 9 Major areas of potential groundwater development. *U.S. Water Resources Council.*

ground water in Salt Lake Valley, virtually inexhaustible . . ." (which could be an alternative source of M&I water).

Fortunately the southwestern deserts, which have the greatest deficiency in surface water supplies, are almost entirely underlain by groundwater. Many other areas of the nation are blessed with groundwater. In fact, almost half the municipal systems in the United States depend upon well water in varying degrees. This "hidden resource" is under-utilized in many areas.

According to David H. Howell, professor emeritus at North Carolina State, and James C. Warman, director of the Water Resources Research Institute at Auburn University:

Groundwater represents the principal domestic water supply for the majority of the people living in the Southeast. With the exception of Florida, there is a general view that groundwater is not sufficiently utilized for domestic supplies. This is attributed to a lack of reliable data on groundwater yields and insufficient familiarity with groundwater development on the part of engineers, lawyers and regulatory agencies.

Like Arizona, Florida is one of America's fastest growing states. It is like Arizona in other ways. According to an 1982 article in the American Society of Civil Engineers *Journal*, the 1970-71 drought gave the public and many elected officials the impression that southern Florida was approaching its carrying capacity from a water supply standpoint. The article notes that recent studies show that:

> . . . from a long-term viewpoint, growth in South Florida need not be constrained by potable water resource availability. Difficult decisions will be required to balance environmental trade-offs and costs, but the resource is there; it is renewable, and it can be economically developed.

In New Jersey, the extensive groundwater resources in the southern and central part of the state have resulted in positive implications for the environment. Concerns that development might impair the recharge capability of this sandy aquifer led the state to purchase the 150-square-mile Wharton Tract in 1954. More recently the Pinelands National Reserve has been designed to encompass nearly a million acres in the Atlantic Coastal Plain of central New Jersey. Collaterally, the unique flora and fauna of the area, some of which are endangered, have been preserved.

Obviously there are adequate water supplies available in the nation, even in our most arid states, to support populations well beyond any reasonable projections. Thus any city in the area that claims water shortage must be admitting that its laws and policies are the problem. Laws and policies can always be changed, and this could be the quickest and least expensive way to solve most crises involving water for personal use. But politics are often an almost insurmountable obstacle.

II. POLITICS AND ALFALFA IN THE DESERT

5. Man-Made Shortages

The City of Tucson's 1974 report on the Central Arizona Project provides the most concise explanation of Arizona's water problem: "Arizona's water supply is not so much one of a limited amount of water, it is a legal problem. . . ." In the words of that unforgettable comic strip character Pogo: "We have met the enemy and they is us."

The lifeline of lakes and rivers that provide the water for the Phoenix area's less than 2 million residents could meet the needs of all of New York City's 7 million people, according to a TV documentary in the early 1970s. In spite of this, in 1977 a headline of Phoenix's leading newspaper proclaimed that the north side of that city was "running dry." In 1981 another headline proposed a ban on new industry in the same area. The cause of this alleged predicament is the Salt River Project (SRP).

The SRP is a special district which began as the Salt River Valley Water Users Association in 1903. Its purpose was to provide water to the agricultural lands in the Phoenix area. Today it is the second largest public utility in Arizona. SRP's electrical power operation provides 98% of its total revenues and subsidizes its water operation. Income from SRP's electricity customers averaged $10 million a year through the decade of the '70s and approached $14 million in 1982. It helps keep the price of water so ludicruously low that it is delivered to the land for less than a penny a ton. This means that water, which is supposedly so precious, is cheaper than dirt.

SRP delivers water to the lands within the District's defined boundaries. The rapidly growing areas of north
Phoenix and Scottsdale are outside these boundaries and
are therefore not permitted to consume these surface waters.

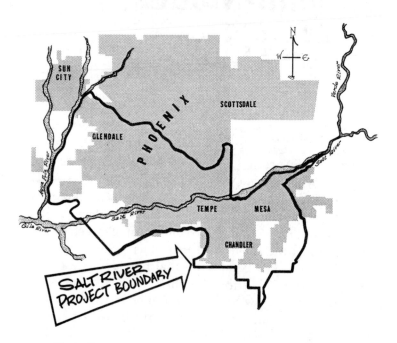

Fig. 10 The Salt River Project and the Phoenix area. *Brian Evans.*

The reason for this is that Arizona's surface water law,
which is typical of surface water laws in the West, is based
on the concept of prior appropriation—first in time, first in
right. As irrigation of the land within the district began in
the 1860's, these lands are entitled to first use of all the
water that flows from the Salt and Verde rivers in a normal
year. Under existing laws and policies, therefore, it is possible that people outside SRP boundaries, including Phoenix
area residents, could run out of water while farmers within
the boundaries continue to grow cotton for export.

The simplest solution to the water problem of metropolitan Phoenix would appear to be to divert some of the SRP
water to those who reside outside the present SRP boundaries. But changing the system is easier said than done. In

her 1978 testimony, the Mayor of Phoenix told Congress that water could not be diverted by changing the boundaries:

Because the Project boundaries were established historically and cannot, I am told, be feasibly expanded at least in this era, a great many of the newer residents of Phoenix are not entitled to domestic use of the waters impounded by the project dams on the Salt and Verde Rivers.

Fig. 11 *Dave Campbell.*

Perhaps the boundaries cannot be expanded. But water *can* be transferred outside those boundaries. Since 1924 SRP has been providing water to an irrigation district just outside its eastern boundary in exchange for improvements to SRP's delivery system. A similar arrangement was arrived at in 1943 with an irrigation district outside SRP's western boundary. The SRP board of directors could just as easily agree to sell Phoenix enough water to service its "off-project" lands. Or, in exchange for water, the city could improve SRP's delivery system by covering the SRP district's open canals or replacing them with pipelines. This would save water by reducing evaporative losses. (It would also save lives, since drownings in open canals are common in Arizona. Needless to say, children are the frequent victims.)

The reason such obvious solutions have not been implemented is simple, although very complex in its operation. When the state legislature gave SRP the status of a municipality in 1934, it created a city with its associated powers. including that of condemning land. This removed SRP from the control of the Corporation Commission, which regulates

Arizona's other utilities, thus creating an unregulated monopoly, controlled only by SRP's board of directors.

Historically SRP directors have been large landholders who represent agricultural interests. For obvious reasons they want to retain the abundant supplies of low cost water which they've been able to obtain by subsidizing their water operations with revenues from the sale of electricity. Only owners of property that is within SRP boundaries are permitted to vote for SRP directors, and voting is on the basis of one acre—one vote. Thus the owner of 100 acres of agricultural land has 100 votes, and he has a strong incentive to go to the polls since his livelihood depends upon the abundant supply of cheap water provided by the present system. Urban interests would have to get 500 owners of the typical fifth-of-an-acre city lot to equal the farmer's one vote. The average Phoenician doesn't understand the system and has little incentive to vote.

Additional inequities exist. Large areas outside SRP boundaries receive SRP energy but are not permitted to vote. Apartment dwellers and other renters, who use considerable amounts of energy, are not allowed to vote. Many property owners within SRP boundaries receive energy from another utility but enjoy low water rates through the subsidy from their neighbors' SRP electric bills. Few politicians are likely to take on such a labyrinthine system, especially since public apathy (due to understandable ignorance) has traditionally been high and voter turnout low.

This is the kind of situation that leads to lawsuits. The Arizona Center for Law in the Public Interest sued to change the voting arrangements, won in the U.S. District Court, and the decision was affirmed by the U.S. Court of Appeals. Early in 1981, however, the U.S. Supreme Court in a 5-4 decision overturned the lower courts and held that the voting arrangement of the SRP is constitutional. That decision was severely criticized in 1982 by the *Arizona State Law Journal.* It noted that the court equated SRP with California's Tulare Lake District, which served a rural population of 73 and provided no electrical power. More than three quarters of the land was owned by four corporations. The *Journal* felt the Supreme Court should have compared SRP with the

Imperial Irrigation District in California, since both provide water and electricity to thousands of urban residents. In 1976 the California Supreme Court noted the difference between Tulare and Imperial and held that property was an invalid qualification for holding office and voting in the latter case.

Land Use

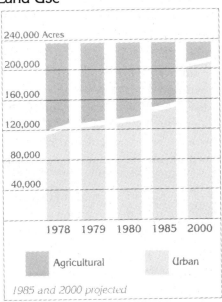

Fig. 12 Projected urbanization of the Salt River Project area. *Salt River Project.*

Due to escalating energy costs, an irate citizenry forced the Arizona legislature in 1976 to add four new directors to the ten member SRP Board. These are elected on a one man–one vote basis. At least two of the ten SRP election districts have been heavily urbanized. Several others will be urban dominated in the near future as the SRP area is urbanized. Thus the problem should ultimately be overcome but not before billions of dollars have been spent on the Central Arizona Project.

The city of Scottsdale, on the northeast border of Phoenix, commissioned an engineering firm in 1975 to analyze its water resources. The engineers found the water supply adequate for those portions of the city within SRP but con-

cluded that the city would not have an adequate supply
outside SRP's boundaries by the year 2000 unless:

. . .groundwater is uneconomically mined, exportation of water
from the Salt River Reservoir District becomes possible, or water
from the Colorado River is imported via the Central Arizona
Project.

We saw in the last chapter that there is groundwater under
the Phoenix area within 1200 feet of the surface adequate
to last several centuries. Since CAP would pump water 1200
feet uphill to Phoenix, groundwater mining should be more
economical than CAP water for several centuries. But the
politicians chose the CAP route to solve the artificial water
shortage. Phoenix simply estimated its future growth outside
SRP boundaries and ordered CAP water accordingly. In
what can be considered poetic justice, water-rich SRP residents will have their property taxes and water rates increased to help pay for this multibillion dollar project which
they don't need.

Informing the citizenry of this situation could conceivably
lead to a change in SRP policy or to revised Arizona statutes.
Instead, the City of Phoenix gives tens of thousands of tax
dollars to the CAP Association to promote the importation
of more water.

Dean Mann in his 1963 book, *The Politics of Water in
Arizona*, explains where the CAP association gets most of
its funds: "Irrigation districts, industries, professional, agricultural, financial, and business interests all contribute
according to the nature and amount of interest involved."
SRP's man-made shortage permit those promoters of the
CAP to use the slogan "Water for People" to sell this expensive project to an uninformed citizenry, and the raid on the
federal treasury continues.

That these shenanigans occur elsewhere in the nation is
shown by the following statement by University of Utah
professors of economics, which appeared in a 1979 professional journal:

To drum up support for water development that is obviously not
urgent, they rely on the Western axiom that water is scarce and
that it is not possible to have too much water development. The

important role played in water development by Chamber of Commerce and other civic promoters since 1945 suggests that their primary interest has been in federal stimulation of local growth. The Weber Basin Project and the Teton Dam are cases in point. In fact, heavy propaganda efforts were financed by these groups and individuals. Expanded water supplies are just an acceptable and available window dressing.

Most Americans are aware that the ill-fated Teton Dam is in Idaho. The Weber Basin Project is in Utah.

The federal government is spending more than a billion dollars to build the Central Utah Project to bring more water to the Salt Lake City area. This is not Utah's only analogy to Arizona. Comments in a letter from R. Paul Van Dam, Salt Lake County Attorney, to the Board of County Commissioners on July 5, 1977, would lead one to conclude that Salt Lake City's water problems are not dissimilar to those in the Phoenix area: "I am convinced, from the results of our study thus far, that institutional management, not water scarcity, is the number one issue in the water supply problem for Salt Lake Valley."

Similar institutional problems led to the Corps of Engineers to conclude that the Washington, D.C., area faced a water shortage by 1980. A 1977 restudy concluded that the area was not short of water if it could efficiently use the already available local storage. In July 1982 eight separate agreements among various agencies were signed, assuring adequate water supplies into the next century. Compared to previously evaluated plans, which included as many as 16 major reservoirs, this regional cooperation potentially saved between $200 million and $1 billion.

It certainly seems paradoxical that the great conservative states of Arizona and Utah look to the federal government rather than change their local laws while the much more "liberal" Washington, D.C., area solved its problem locally. Colorado, which is considered rather liberal, has adjusted its laws to facilitate the transfer of water rights. On the other hand, the Texas legislature in 1980 subjected special districts, including those dealing with water, to statewide regulatory agency jurisdiction. New York City does not require the installation of water meters in residential buildings. Thus there is no incentive to conserve water and much is wasted.

Northeastern and midwestern states are now clamoring for federal funds to repair their antiquated water systems, citing massive federal expenditures for western water projects as justification for increasing their share of the federal water pie. It is interesting to note that in 1957 the federal government financed only 10% of state and local public works investments but that by 1980 this had reached 40%. At the 1982 National Water Symposium ". . .all agreed that moving a greater share of power to the local and state level would be a healthy step," but the report added that this would be difficult since "grants for public works projects remain a basic source of power for members of Congress— something that will probably not willingly be surrendered." Cost-sharing proposals under the Reagan administration, especially where the local entity is required to provide a large down-payment, could well signal a return to local responsibility and local solutions to local problems.

The Arizona State University *Law Journal* points out that special government districts like SRP are the most numerous type of government in the United States but constitute the "dark continent of American politics." Included are such entities as the Port Authorities of New York and New Jersey. There are more than 900 special districts engaged in water "conservation" and irrigation, 95% of which are in the West. They distribute about one-half of all water used in the West.

Most irrigation districts were reorganized from some form of private enterprise. Their creation under state law qualifies their property and bonds for exemption from not only state but federal taxation. The U.S. Treasury has estimated that tax-exempt financing is even more expensive to the federal government than a direct interest subsidy.

There are of course many uses for water other than supplying the needs of cities. Producing food is one, and we will take a look at agriculture next.

6. Water for Food

According to the Second National Water Assessment by the U.S. Water Resources Council, in 1978, more than 80% of the nation's fresh water was consumed by irrigated agriculture, and the 17 arid western states accounted for more than 90% of this irrigated agriculture. These, of course, are the states that have a natural water deficiency.

Here then is where we should look for the water crisis. Is all this irrigation necessary? If not, then we should be able to eliminate, or at least alleviate, the projected crisis. But many believe we need all the food we can grow to feed a starving world or to stave off hunger in our own country. Others claim we should produce all the crops we can to keep food prices low or that all this irrigated agriculture is necessary to their local economy. Some Americans believe we are running out of farmland or are urbanizing our prime farmlands and therefore should preserve all the cropland we now have.

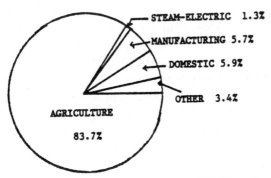

Fig. 13 Water consumption in America. *U.S. Water Resources Council.*

In its 1982 briefing, the Hunger Project summarized the world food picture as follows:

Just in grain alone, the world currently produces more than enough to adequately feed everyone now and everyone expected to be alive in the year 2000. Our current total world food production, if it were equally distributed, could feed more than 7 billion people.

The present world population of 4.5 billion is projected to reach 5.5 to 6 billion by 2000 A.D..

American farmers are among the most productive on the planet; the U.S. has been called the breadbasket of the world. But the productivity of America's farmlands is not the solution to world hunger. As Arthur Simon, executive director of "Bread for the World," emphasizes: "Hunger is almost certain to stalk the poor countries until they increase substantially their own food production." Politics and economic complexities, not shortages, prevent the equitable distribution of food.

Our nation is blessed by an overabundance of food, so more production is not the answer to any hunger problem we may have. In fact, farmers are being paid not to grow crops. The surplus crops include feed grains, wheat, cotton, and rice. In 1983 America paid farmers not to grow these crops on 82 million acres. This means that approximately a fifth of our nation's croplands was "set-aside." The set-aside payments are made to farmers either in tax dollars or in crops—crops that tax moneys bought in previous years to keep prices high.

Claims that government subsidy programs to stimulate agricultural production have benefitted the consumer by keeping prices low were refuted as far back as the 1960s. Economist Charles Schultze noted that during the period 1964-69 the government program increased the price of food by 4% each year above what it otherwise would have been. Texas A&M agricultural economist Bruce L. Gardner wrote in his 1981 book, *The Governing of Agriculture*, that the programs cost the taxpayer $1.4 billion and cost consumers another $5.9 billion in fiscal year 1978/79. He also noted that the gain to producers was $6.4 billion. Purdue professor emeritus Dan Paarlberg, an agricultural economist under

Presidents Eisenhower, Nixon, and Ford, wrote in 1982 that the government programs resulted in the United States losing markets for its exports and were costly to consumers and taxpayers.

Few were prepared for the massive outlay of tax dollars that took place in 1983. In its July 25, 1983, issue, *Newsweek* magazine summarized the situation: "The statistics are boggling: government subsidies to farmers will explode to $21 billion this year. Even more amazing is that these subsidies will just about equal the total earnings of American farmers this year."

The claim is often made that irrigated agriculture makes a significant contribution to state or local economics. Such claims are generally associated with attempts to justify additional water projects by government agencies like the U.S. Bureau of Reclamation (BuRec) and the Corps of Engineers (COE). This claim was refuted by the University of Utah economists in their 1982 paper:

> . . . post-1950 water investments in the Intermountain West and in the Upper Missouri Basin, undertaken by BuRec or COE, have had no statistically significant impact on income, per capita income, employment, or gross sales, when compared with companion areas that did not enjoy such investment.

This finding is easier to understand by looking at the results of a 1974 Utah State Water Engineers Office study. It shows the value added to the state's economy and the increased employment provided through the use of the same increment of water by various sectors in that state. From the following table it should be obvious that agricultural uses of water add comparatively little value to the local economy:

Table 2: Relative Productivity of Water in Utah.

Economic Sector	Valued Added ($/AF)	Employment (in Thous.)
Agriculture	5,600	2
Food Manufacturing	18,800	2
Mining (metals)	277,000	15
Metal Manufacturing	758,500	7
Utilities	867,500	11
Business Services	11,147,500	123
Communications	10,399,000	136

It has been argued that we need as much irrigated farmland as possible because urban development is consuming prime land. Although it is true that we are losing some cropland to the cities, the amount is insignificant compared to all of the farmland in the nation. As Julian Simon, a professor of economics and business administration at the University of Illinois pointed out in the July 27, 1980, issue of *Science*: "All the land used for urban areas plus roadways totals less than 3% of the area of the United States. . . . The U.S. Department of Agriculture says 'we are in no danger of running out of farmland.'" Only 67% of our best land is used to grow crops. Much of the rest is in pasture, which can be readily provided on poorer land. Irrigating new lands in the West and contributing to a water crisis in the process can hardly be justified by the claim of farmland shortages elsewhere.

Table 3: Use of Prime Farmland in 1977 (Soil Conservation Service)

Land Use	Acres (millions)	Percent
Cropland	230	67
Native pasture and Pastureland	40	12
Rangeland	22	6
Forest land	42	12
Other land	11	3
Total	345	100

Indeed, just as irrigated land has increased in the West, land under cultivation has decreased in other parts of the country, primarily the humid East and South. Figure 15 shows the dramatic shift in U.S. cropland that took place between 1944 and 1964. Professor Simon in his Heritage Foundation paper shows that this trend continued through 1975, noting that the biggest loss of cropland was in the South. He gives the reason for this as follows: ". . . the land story of the South in recent decades has been the massive abandonment of cropland to forest and to scrubland simply because it is no longer economical to farm cotton and similar crops." By 1981 the seven southeastern states accounted for

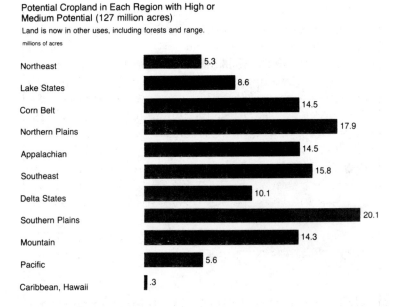

Potential Cropland in Each Region with High or
Medium Potential (127 million acres)

Land is now in other uses, including forests and range.

millions of acres

Northeast	5.3
Lake States	8.6
Corn Belt	14.5
Northern Plains	17.9
Appalachian	14.5
Southeast	15.8
Delta States	10.1
Southern Plains	20.1
Mountain	14.3
Pacific	5.6
Caribbean, Hawaii	.3

Fig. 14 Potential cropland in America. *Soil Conservation Service.*

only 8% of the nation's cotton acreage, while 16% of our cotton acreage was in Arizona, California, and New Mexico.

The shift in cropland reveals a sinister cause and effect relationship to others who have looked more deeply into this situation. They suggest that it is the federal government that has made this southern farming uneconomical. For decades the U.S. Bureau of Reclamation has been spending billions of tax dollars to irrigate the West. The effect of this subsidy on the rest of the nation is summarized by agricultural economists Howe and Easter in their 1972 study, *Interbasin Transfers of Water*:

Substantial evidence of production displacement by western irrigated agriculture has been presented (in this study) suggesting that increased reclamation irrigation over the period 1944-1964 has displaced millions of acres of farm land in nonreclamation areas.

Howe and Easter are even more specific on the economics of growing cotton:

Data from an analysis of the costs of producing upland cotton in the United States indicate that Southern California and Southwest

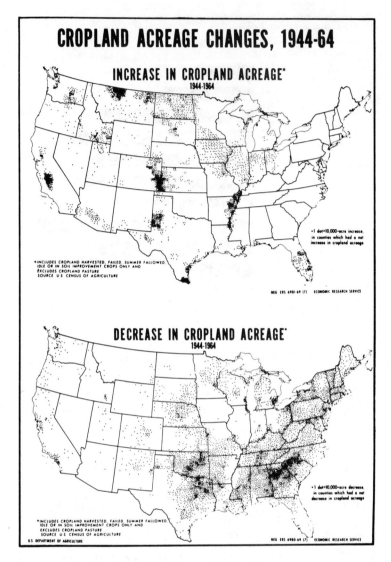

Fig. 15 *U.S. Department of Agriculture.*

Arizona are enabled to stay in production at lower cotton prices only because of the low price they pay for reclamation irrigation water. . . . If irrigators . . . had to pay the average cost of providing new water, their costs of production would be raised substantially and . . . there would be an average loss ranging from $36 to $96 per bale. . . .

In December 1981 M. Rupert Cutler, senior vice president

of the National Audubon Society and former assistant secretary of agriculture during the Carter Administration, told
the National Association of Manufacturers:

Cheap water. That's why cotton is grown in the West, where
water is so limited. There's no reason why the cotton industry
can't move back to the Southeast, where there's a surplus water
supply.

WHO CONSUMES THE WATER

AND WHERE IT COMES FROM

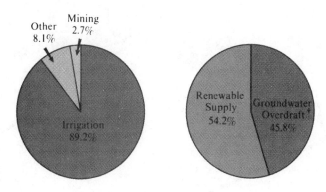

† *Groundwater used but not replaced
resulting in a declining water table.*

Fig. 16 Arizona water consumption. *Arizona Water Commission.*

Eighty-nine percent of Arizona's water is consumed by
agriculture. Mines consume less than 3%. All other uses—
cities, industry, etc.—consume only 8%. Forty-six percent
of all water consumed is from groundwater mining, which
is obviously attributable to agriculture. This profligate use
of water by the agribusiness industry has been acceptable
by Arizona's citizens due to several misconceptions, one of
the most absurd of which is that Arizona's farms are needed
to feed Arizonans.

"Almost none of the food produced in Arizona is directly
consumed by Arizona. In fact, very little of the irrigated
acreage in Arizona is devoted to 'food' crops." So wrote a
noted agricultural economist at the University of Arizona.
Only a small portion of Arizona's farmland is in vegetables,

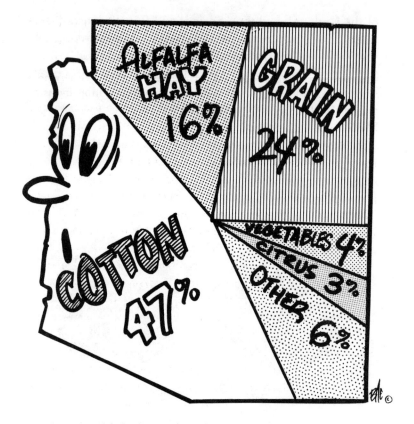

ARIZONA'S CROPLAND USE
1980

Fig. 17 Arizona's Cropland Use, 1980. *Brian Evans and U.S. Department of Agriculture.*

even though that crop consumes little water. Citrus accounts for an even smaller percentage of the state's acreage.

Almost half of the state's agricultural acreage is in cotton, which is certainly not an edible crop. The water consumption of this one crop is equal to the amount of groundwater mined in the state each year. Almost all of Arizona's cotton is exported to areas with cheap labor, primarily the Far East, from where much of it is then sold back to us as finished goods.

Alfalfa is the most blatant water user. It consumes 74 inches per acre per year, while lettuce, at the other extreme, consumes only 8 inches. As a result, alfalfa hay consumes 28% of the state's water annually while representing only 16% of its irrigated acreage. Approximately one-third of this hay is exported while another third is used to feed cattle, most of which is then exported to California.

Not surprisingly, an increasing number of people are questioning the wisdom of growing surplus crops and hay in the desert. The folly is recognized even by the foreign press. The prestigious London *Economist* concluded in its May 14, 1983, article entitled "American Survey: Water in the West" that "if Westerners did not farm, even the driest states would not worry much about water."

Defense of present practices is also based on a superficially more plausible assumption, that Arizona's agriculture is necessary to Arizona's economy. Although this was the case in Arizona's early days—when cotton, copper, citrus, and cattle were Arizona's economy—it is simply no longer true. Between 1950 and 1960 manufacturing overtook agriculture as a leading source of Arizona's personal income and this dramatic shift is revealed in other indicators. In 1960 ag-

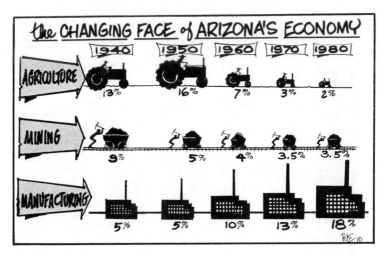

Fig. 18 Comparison of personal income from three Arizona industries. *Brian Evans and U.S. Department of Commerce.*

riculture accounted for 7% of Arizona's Real Gross State Product; it decreased to 4% by 1970. Farmers and farm workers accounted for only 2.8% of Arizona's employment in 1970.

By 1980 agriculture contributed only 2% to the state's personal income, while consuming 89% of Arizona's water. All other uses of water account for 98% of Arizona's personal income, while consuming only 11% of its water. Tourism and travel expenditures alone amounted to four times the value of crop production in 1980, and an Arizona bank vice president told the 1981 Arizona Economic Forum: "By the year 2000, tourism is expected to be the single largest industry in Arizona."

Figure 19, adapted from a 1973 study by University of Arizona agricultural economists Kelso, Martin, and Mack, dramatically shows the large amounts of water required by Arizona agriculture to produce $1,000 worth of finished product. Equally dramatic is the comparison between irrigated agriculture and mining shown in Figure 20. This is from a brochure entitled "Arizona Water: What its Use for

Fig. 19 Relative productivity of water in Arizona. *Brian Evans and Kelso, Martin, and Mack.*

Mining and Irrigation Means to the State of Arizona and its Citizens," which was distributed by the Arizona State AFL-CIO in 1980. Both of these graphs speak for themselves and should make it obvious that a reduction in the state's irrigated agriculture would have no earthshaking effect on Arizona's economy. Even if agriculture in Arizona gradually

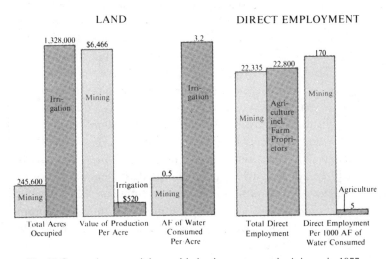

Fig. 20 Comparison on mining and irrigation water use in Arizona in 1977.

decreases by 18% due to the rising cost of groundwater as University of Arizona economists predict, the resulting decline in Arizona personal income will be less than one tenth of one percent. This minute decline would be caused by a reduction in the water-consumptive but low-value-producing crops such as alfalfa.

The increased cost of groundwater will not be due to a lack of water, *per se*, for it will be many centuries before the underground reservoir "runs dry". Even if the present rate of mining this resource continues, there is enough water in storage under the southern deserts of Arizona to permit agriculture to remain in "business as usual" for many centuries. The problem is one of simple economics. As the groundwater level lowers, wells will have to be drilled deeper, and the energy to pump water will become more expensive. Agribusiness simply cannot afford to grow low-valued crops with expensive water.

But so far, Arizona agriculture has been steadily increasing its acreage. It reached one million acres in 1949, right after Arizona passed its first groundwater law in a half-hearted attempt to control the state's increasing groundwater overdraft. There has been a steady increase since then. In 1980 it was 1.3 milion—a 10% increase since 1970.

During that same decade of the '70s, Arizona experienced a 50% increase in population. While much of the resulting urbanization has taken place on prime farmland, this was more than replaced by new farmland coming into production. This is not surprising since there are more than 30 million acres of irrigable land in Arizona. Very little of this land is classified as "prime" by the U.S. Department of Agriculture, simply because that designation requires the land to have a dependable water supply. As a result the Department can classify as "prime" only those lands presently under irrigation, even though adjacent parcels may have exactly the same characteristics but no water rights.

Fears of eliminating prime farmland have led to suggestions that people should live in the mountains so that farming can continue in the valleys. Building roads, sewer and water lines, and homes in these rocky areas would result in tremendous increases in housing costs for urban residents. Fortunately, the free market was allowed to operate. Farmers simply moved further out, drilled new wells and thus created prime farmland.

Rather than letting the market place determine the "highest and best" use of existing water supplies, Arizona embarked on the typical western appoach—import more water from somewhere else. One of Arizona's leading conservative politicians even testified before the U.S. Congress when the Central Arizona Project was in trouble in 1977 that "Arizona needs more water at any price." Few would make this statement about gold, oil, or virtually any other commodity. It typifies the "water is different" syndrome. It could be true if Arizonans were going to die of thirst—but we have seen that is far from the case. It could also be true if there were no "free market" in water—and that is more nearly the case.

The concept of continually bringing in more water was pioneered by southern California in the early part of this century—first from the Owens Valley, then from the Colorado River. In his 1982 book, *Water and Power*, William Kahrl discusses that era with references to the U.S. Bureau of Reclamation's duplicity in dealing with contending interests. He also cites the manipulations of the electorate by the Los Angeles Department of Water and Power, which terrorized taxpayers with manufactured threats of drought in order to get them to foot the bill for water delivery systems they did not need. Behind all this he found the financial wheeling and dealing of big-time real estate speculators and media czars. This provided the background for the well known Hollywood movie *Chinatown*, starring Jack Nicholson and Faye Dunaway.

How does agriculture remain in business in the face of competition from the other more profitable sectors of Arizona's economy? It has a virtual monopoly on surface water rights, which are attached to the land. If a manufacturer wanted to buy the water being used on a cotton or alfalfa farm, it would be necessary to buy the entire farm. Also, as we saw earlier, water from the Salt River Project is dirt cheap since it is subsidized by the urban energy user. And agriculture is also subsidized by very low property tax rates.

This subsidy is less visible than others. Agricultural land has a lower assessment ratio than any other business in Arizona. For tax purposes it is valued even lower than resi-

Fig. 21 *Dave Campbell.*

dential land. A 1979 study by the Arizona Department of Revenue showed that the average value for tax purposes on a single-family home was $33,958, while the sales value was $38,958. Cropland was valued at $18,659 although it sold for an average $100,194.

This vast discrepancy is a result of agricultural land being valued on the basis on production, while all other land is assessed on the full cash value. This encourages the owner of agricultural land near a city to grow less valuable crops, especially in the environs of a rapidly growing city where land values are skyrocketing. A much publicized case in the Phoenix area involved a landowner who ran a few sheep across his land in an unsuccessful attempt to get agricultural classification.

In the Phoenix area between 1976 and 1978, homes were valued at 89% of full cash value while field crops were valued at 18.6%. Vacant land was valued at 21.5% to 37%. This obviously encourages a developer to keep his land under cultivation while waiting for urbanization to increase its value. In fact, since value is based upon production, he would do well to grow the cheapest crop that can be grown most easily. This (and cheap water) could explain why one quarter of the harvested cropland in the Salt River Project area is in alfalfa. It is an easily mechanized crop, requiring little labor.

As we have seen, alfalfa is also the thirstiest crop. Arizona's 200,000 acres of alfalfa, with its consumption of more than 6 feet per acre, accounts for 1.2 million acre feet—the expected water supply of the Central Arizona Project. In light of the cost of that project, one must wonder about the wisdom of growing hay in central Arizona deserts. Thus, the tax policy could be contributing to the groundwater overdraft, which helps promote construction of the CAP, which will further increase taxes. All non-agricultural interests are also paying increased taxes to make up for taxes agribusiness is not paying.

These property tax subsidies might make sense if they were part of a plan to maintain agriculture for aesthetic reasons. The law makes no requirement, however, that the land remain in farms. In California the Williamson Plan defers taxes on farmlands but requires repayment if the lands are sold within a certain number of years. Many urbanites would probably prefer a greenbelt of farmlands surrounding their cities, and wastewater from urban areas could provide the tool to implement such a plan.

The Buckeye Irrigation District just west of Phoenix had been pumping the equivalent of 10% of the CAP's annual supply. In 1962 they began receiving wastewater from Phoenix and by 1983 it constituted 60% of their water supply. They have discovered that wastewater irrigated crops return a greater yield per acre than crops grown with pump water plus fertilizer. But by the late 1980s this water will be used to cool the Palo Verde Nuclear Power Plant. This is unfortunate since better planning might have resulted in energy savings, and the maintenance of an agricultural greenbelt around the Phoenix area.

There is actually an excess of groundwater in the Buckeye Irrigation District. This results in waterlogging, where the roots of the crops are essentially drowned since the groundwater is so close to the surface. As a result, the district operates pumps around the clock to lower the water levels. The planners of the Palo Verde Plant could have pumped this groundwater to cool their plant. Instead they plan to use the wastewater—after removing the nutrients!

Conservation measures by Arizona agriculture are all too rare. In fact, the agribusiness seems more interested in getting urban residents to conserve water. In 1982 the Arizona Cotton Growers Association ran "Arizona Needs Water" advertisements in the state's largest newspaper in an attempt to educate the city people and sell them water saving shower heads for $6.50. Their brochure even encourages urbanites to put a brick in the toilet.

III. CONSERVATION

7. A Brick in the Toilet

Agriculture consumes 89% of the water in the West. As it is estimated that a 7% reduction in agricultural water use in the West would support a 100% increase in all other uses, surely water conservation efforts would be misdirected if they did not concentrate on agricultural use.

California's 1976-77 drought provides the perfect paradox of urban and agricultural conservation. In that state, urban uses consume only 6% of the water, compared to 91% for agriculture. According to the 1978 *California Water Atlas*, the acreage of alfalfa in that state is the same as the combined irrigated acreage in Arizona. Of the top three crops in California, alfalfa uses 54% of the water while producing only 27% of the value. Grapes use only 15% of the water while producing 40% of the value. During the 1976-77 drought, the acreage in field crops remained virtually unchanged while vegetables, fruit, and nut production actually increased. Urban areas were forced to conserve and in some areas reduced water use by as much as 50%.

In yet another paradox, arid southern California cities reduced their use by only 12% while the more humid cities to the north managed a reduction of 25%. The Marin Municipal Water District, just north of San Francisco, provided the extreme example by reducing its use by 53%.

In Arizona much publicity has been devoted to urban conservation, ranging from the brick in the toilet and low flow showerheads to placards on restaurant tables advertising the water crisis. It is easy to sell a water crisis in the

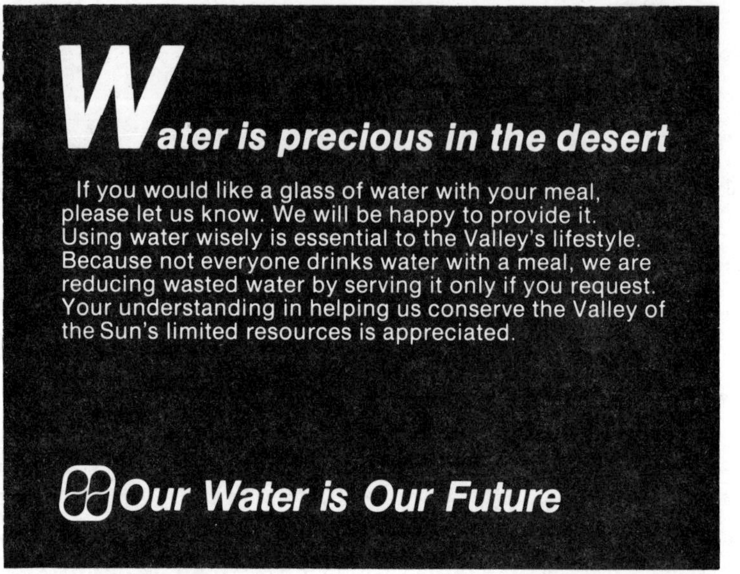

Fig. 22 Typical water conservation restaurant placard. *City of Phoenix*.

desert—and to ignore the real facts. Yet a glance at Figure 23 shows that agriculture is the overwhelming consumer of Arizona water. Just an 8% reduction in agricultural depletion would save as much water as is consumed by all the cities and industries (except mines) in the state. It must be pointed out that the overdraft shown in Figure 23 is the rough equivalent of the cotton grown in Arizona.

To further put the picture in proper perspective, urban areas consume 1.4 acre feet per acre (af/ac), according to the Arizona water commissioner. Agriculture in the Phoenix area consumes 3.6 af/ac. Thus every acre that is urbanized results in a substantial reduction in water use. This led one engineering report to conclude that the groundwater overdraft in the Phoenix area would be eliminated before the turn of the century. Note that this would entail no government involvement; the market would take care of the situation.

Conserving water could of course save urbanites some of their tax money since fewer treatment plants, wells, reservoirs, etc., would be needed. This could be particularly important in areas like Tucson if the rapid rate of urban growth continues. Again conservation measures should be concentrated in areas where they are most effective. Water that is used inside the home can be recycled. Virtually all the water used outside the home is lost through evaporation or transpiration from plants. This is where Tucson achieved its dramatic reduction in water consumption.

As Table 4 from the Arizona Water Commission's 1978 Water Conservation report shows, yard watering represents almost half the residential water use in the state. Here then is the prime arena for urban water conservation.

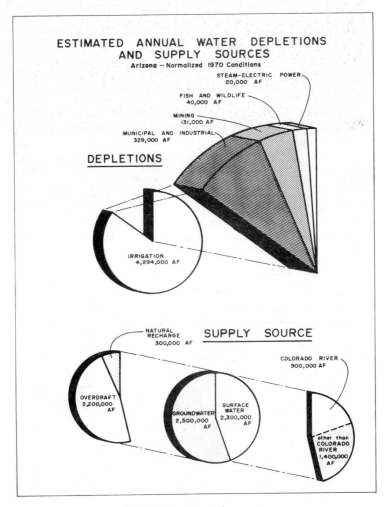

Fig. 23 *Arizona Water Commission.*

**Table 4: Estimated Residential Water Use
Arizona — 1976**

Type of Use	gpcd	AF/YR	Percent
Interior			
Toilet	30.00	77,400	20
Bath	22.00	57,600	15
Laundry and Dishes	14.00	36,000	9
Drinking and Cooking	4.00	9,000	2
Subtotal	70.00	180,000	46
Exterior			
Yard Watering	71.00	179,500	47
Evaporative Coolers	6.00	15,600	4
Swimming Pools	2.00	6,100	2
Other	1.00	4,800	1
Subtotal	80.00	206,000	54
TOTAL	150.00	386,00	100

Conservation of water and energy have a lot in common.
Both are plagued with peak demands, as Figure 46 shows.
Note that the sewer flow is constant, indicating that the
peak is caused primarily by exterior uses of water. It was
a "Beat the Peak" campaign, coupled with large increases

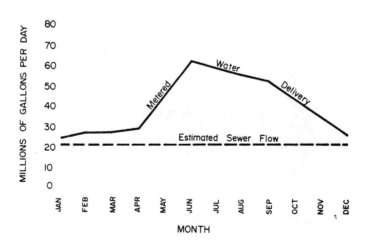

AVERAGE SINGLE-FAMILY RESIDENTIAL WATER USE AND
SEWER DISCHARGE IN TUCSON - 1975

Fig. 24 Peak water usage in Tucson. *Arizona Water Commission.*

in water prices, that permitted Tucson to achieve its water conservation feat.

Like energy, water is responsive to large increases in price. Doubling of water rates permitted Marin County, California, to achieve its water conservation extreme during the 1977 drought. In yet another paradox of our wonderful world of water, water rates are generally higher in the humid East than in the arid West. In an article on "The Future of Water" in the July 1983 *Atlantic Monthly*, Peter Rogers, Gordon McKay Professor of Environmental Engineering, compared eastern and western water rates. He found that arid El Paso charges 53¢ per thousand gallons, and Albuquerque and Los Angles charge 59¢ and 60¢ respectively. In the humid east, Boston charges $1.00 per thousand gallons, while Philadelphia's price is $1.78.

In Arizona, Phoenix and Tucson provide illustrative extremes. Phoenix uses more than twice as much water per person as Tucson does. Tucson's water price is more than double that of Phoenix.

A drive through the desert cities of Phoenix and Tucson provides a visual reflection of prevailing water-use habits. In Tucson, one is never quite sure where the desert ends and the city begins. Drought resistant vegetation is the landscape theme. Driving through Phoenix is like driving through "Any City, U.S.A." when it comes to the landscaping. People seem to have brought their lawns with them when they left the northern climes. Lakes, fountains, and swimming pools are common.

It is obvious that Tucson residents responded to increased water prices by shifting to desert landscaping. By reducing their "lawnscaped" areas, Tucson residents saved water, saved money through reduced water rates, and saved the energy required to pump water and mow lawns. They also helped reduce the humidity which tends to make the hot summers more uncomfortable. Last, but far from least to many allergy sufferers, they reduced the pollen count.

The hot, dry Arizona climate was once considered a haven for tuberculosis sufferers like Doc Holliday. In the 1960s, television commercials advertised a nasal spray as the equivalent of sending your sinuses to Arizona. Since then the amount of pollen in urbanized areas has increased 100%. The slogan is now, if you don't have a sinus problem when you come to Arizona, you'll get one.

Most lawns in the desert southwest are Bermuda grass, which is second only to ragweed as an allergin. Olive and mulberrry trees are the next worst offenders. All are large water users and all have been artificially introduced into the state. Even ragweed is not a native but is found wherever the natural terrain has been disturbed. These plants depend on the airborne pollen dust released by the male for fertilization. Plants that are pollinated by insects produce flowers that are larger, more colorful and fragrant, and won't normally cause allergic reactions.

As a result of all this lawnscaping, Tucson and Phoenix have the worst problems for allergy sufferers in the nation. Tucson's county government passed an ordinance in 1984 prohibiting the sale of olive and mulberry trees and requiring the frequent mowing of Bermuda lawns to prevent the production of pollen.

Claims have been made that desert landscaping will increase energy consumption. While this may be true with the "two cacti and a bunch of gravel" method, desert landscaping need not result in a yard that is hot and dry. Many native trees provide welcome shade, and there are shrubs and ground covers that remain green year-round. With proper selection, the homeowner can have flowers every month of the year.

Tucson has led the way in water conservation by reducing its consumption to 140 gallons per person per day. It can further reduce this, but the major water consumer in the area is agriculture, which accounts for 54% of the depletion. In 1980 more than three quarters of the irrigated land in the area was in cotton and grains, with only 2% devoted to vegetables. Tucson also boasts the world's largest grove of pecans, a tree that is native to the humid southeastern part of our nation.

In the early 1970s, well before the state came to the same conclusion in its groundwater law, Tucson began retiring farmland. This was accomplished at a fraction of the cost of CAP water importation. If the market place was allowed to operate freely, agriculture would be greatly reduced before the CAP or further conservation was implemented.

That Tucson is the largest city in the nation solely dependent upon groundwater is a favorite statement by Arizona politicians in their annual trek to Washington to get more federal tax dollars for the CAP. It sound ominous but, as we've seen, the more relevant question is how long the water in storage underground will last. Besides, the allegation itself is not true. Tucson is the third largest city in the nation, behind Memphis and San Antonio, solely dependent upon groundwater!

As noted previously, the Phoenix area presents a startling contrast to Tucson's desert landscape. Here it is apparent that water waste must be curtailed before other conservation measures can begin. Even the government gives only lip service to conservation, since it constantly waters the grass in highway medians and shoulders and around government buildings. This "lawnscaping" of the Phoenix desert is epitomized by one of the award winning landscapes selected by the Arizona Landscape Contractors' Association. It consists of 30,000 square feet of lawn which takes about five hours to mow.

This profligate use of water is particularly prevalent in the Salt River Project area. Lawns are watered by the same flood irrigation methods and from the same canals as those used by agriculture. According to a July 1981 report by the City of Phoenix, such residential flood irrigation pushes the rate of water use from 230 gpd to about 300 gpd—more than double Tucson's rate. Indeed, it is not unusual to see water flowing down the streets while the sun is shining, as the water floods over the banks bordering each lawn.

The Phoenix area has little incentive for conservation since water is both abundant and cheap. The rapidly growing area outside the Salt River Project boundaries could provide this incentive since they depend on groundwater, like Tucson. In early 1982 Phoenix decided to embark upon a conservation program in order to reduce water consumption in this area.

Unfortunately, any water conserved by Phoenix residents within the SRP boundary cannot be consumed by those residents outside the boundaries where the artificial water shortage exists. SRP does permit its water to be delivered to these "off-project" residents, but it is only a loan. The cities must pump water from wells that are off-project and return it to the SRP canals, resulting in unnecessary energy consumption. The resultant lowering of the groundwater leads to land subsidence, which is discussed in detail in the appendix. All this of course leads to a demand for CAP water.

Under present policy, conservation by residents within the project boundary will not benefit their "off-project" neighbors. If free transferability of water was allowed, the market place could solve the artificial shortage while encouraging conservation. The cities could extend an offer to all residents within the boundary to buy or lease water. If the price was high enough, owners of water rights would be encouraged to conserve, and the resulting water would be supplied to off-project lands.

Note that this approach does not need to affect existing water rights. The right still belongs to the land within the project. Law determines who owns property, but the owner determines how to use it. It is commonplace in our society for the owner of a house to rent it or the owner of a car to lease it.

The open canals through which SRP delivers water próvide other opportunities for conservation. First, there is the energy-wasteful practice whereby SRP pumps groundwater into canals and delivers it as surface water. Since surface water is priced much lower than pump water, this has obviously been to the advantage of large landowners, but it subjects the water to evaporative losses. In addition, millions of dollars have been spent to line thousands of miles with concrete to prevent seepage. This seepage is not a true loss of water for it eventually reaches the underground reservoirs.

Evaporation from the water surface of an open channel is a true loss to the system, so it would surely seem a better investment to cover the canals. Since the Arizona Supreme Court reversed a long-term ruling that water was more valuable than human life, canal owners are now liable when children drown in their canals. This liability should encourage covering canals, which will save water as well as lives. CAP water will, of course, be delivered in even larger open canals.

An additional and more substantial concern regarding evaporation arises from the evaporative losses of the huge reservoirs in Arizona. In the low desert near Phoenix, more than 10 feet of water can be evaporated from the surface of the large lakes each year. If all six SRP reservoirs on the Salt and Verde Rivers were full, this could amount to an annual loss of more than 200,000 acre feet. This is additionally significant when we consider that the average annual water supply from the reservoirs, according to the Arizona Water Commission, is less than one million acre feet. These lakes are not often full, so the average annual loss is 70,000 acre feet. Perhaps it would be wise to make sure the lakes do not remain full during the hot, dry summers by releasing water from the dams to recharge the groundwater and prevent those excessive evaporative losses.

Even more significant are the losses from Lake Mead and other reservoirs on the Colorado River. In the Lower Basin lakes alone, annual evaporation is equivalent to the amount of water the CAP is supposed to supply each year. In the 17 western states, large reservoirs evaporate more than 12 million acre feet each year, according to a 1962 U.S. Geological Survey report. Many new dams have been built since then. Congress has authorized four new, large reservoirs as part of the CAP, which will add to the losses.

The evaporation of this pure, almost distilled, water affects the CAP in other ways—it increases the salinity of the remaining water supplies. CAP water will contain 50% more salts than present surface water supplies in the Phoenix and Tucson areas. Thus, in this era when billions of dollars are being spent to clean up the nation's water, the Bureau of Reclamation is planning a project that will, unfortunately, further pollute central Arizona's water supply.

8. Dripping, Flooding and Wasting

Most of the discussion of agricultural water conservation concentrates on drip irrigation, sprinklers, and other methods of applying water. However, the most effective method would be the selection of crops that have minimum water requirements. Lettuce and other vegetables in general are low-water consumptive — and high value — crops, yet they constituted less than 5% of Arizona's 1980 irrigated acreage. Alfalfa, a high-water using, low-value crop, accounted for almost 16% of the cropland. Agricultural researchers have suggested growing other crops in the desert which are more adaptable. Notable among these are jojoba, a substitute for sperm whale oil; guyayule, a rubber producer; buffalo gourds, a source of protein; and various oil-producing plants. Since these are native plants, they can get by on very little water.

Among the various methods of delivering water to crops, drip irrigation systems are by far the most efficient since they irrigate only the plant. Their drawback is the extensive

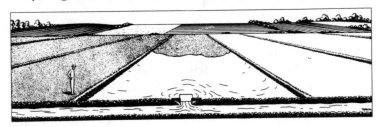

Fig. 25 Flood irrigation. *Soil Conservation Service.*

piping system which generally limits their use to perennial crops like citrus. However, drip irrigation has been used successfully on vegetables and even on cotton. One farmer reported a 40% water saving, with 33% less fertilizer, while doubling his cotton production.

The most popular method of distributing irrigation water in Arizona is flood irrigation. Water is released from the upper end of a field and allowed to "flood" the entire parcel. As a result, several inches of water are standing at the upper end of the field before water reaches the lower end. Laser leveling of the field and shorter "runs", however, can result in more than 90% efficiency.

Sprinkler systems can equal this efficiency, but the energy costs are much higher. Center pivot sprinklers are becoming quite popular and result in the circular fields often seen from the air. Their major claim to fame seems to be the savings in labor, although they are particularly useful in sandy soils.

Conservation means more than the reduction in the amount of water used however. It has been defined as the wise use of our resources. Thus far we have been referring to the one-time use of our water resources, but water is not necessarily destroyed through usage. It can often be reused many times. Nationally only 30 to 40 percent of the water used in urban areas is actually consumed. Most of the water is returned to the system as wastewater.

Presently half of the water used by the city of Tucson becomes wastewater. Farmers are becoming increasingly aware that its use will save them money and even increase their production. An irrigation district in the Tucson vicinity has estimated that the present worth of benefits from substituting 40% of its pump water with wastewater was in excess of $4 million.

The wastes in this water are nutrients to the plant community. In the Tucson area, for example, there are 37 pounds of phosphate in each acre foot of wastewater. Phosphate is one of the principal crop fertilizers, and it has been predicted that the U.S. supply of phosphate rock could run out by 2000 A.D.. An acre foot of Tucson's wastewater also contains 76 pounds of nitrogen.

Non-edible crops, which constitute more than 90% of Arizona's irrigated acreage, are the ideal recipients of this wastewater. During years of water supply shortages, the use of wastewater from the cities will be required to satisfy almost one third of the Indian CAP allocation. This could be used to grow alfalfa to feed livestock. It could also be used to grow American Pima cotton, which would be appropriate since it was originally grown by Arizona's Pima Indians. This long staple cotton is not easily mechanized and constitutes less than 7% of Arizona's cotton acreage.

Agriculture in central Arizona will probably be gradually reduced. Conservation might slow down this reduction, and the state law now requires conservation. However, other state policies—ranging from subsidized water and energy to water rights and property taxes—actually encourage the profligate use of water.

Conservation through improved delivery systems is quite expensive. For example, drip systems cost roughly $1,000 an acre. With surface water priced at less than $10 an acre foot, the savings of one or two acre feet hardly makes the system worthwhile. But with increased depth to groundwater and increased energy prices, an increasing number of these systems are being installed.

Obviously the price of water is one of the major obstacles to conservation. Another major obstacle is water law. The Western rule of prior appropriation grants a perpetual right to that land which first puts water to beneficial use. Thus a settler who began irrigating in Phoenix in 1869 established the water right for his land forever, even though he no longer owns the land and both he and his children are dead.

If a water right is not used for a period of five years, it is lost and can be appropriated by others. As a result, there is no incentive to conserve. In fact, the law seems to encourage the continuation of the growth of high water-consuming crops. Since much of the value of desert land is dependent on water, it makes sense to maintain the highest water right possible by growing water consumptive crops. To conserve water is to lose it! This disincentive can be remedied by the simple policy of permitting the free-market transfer of water. This would allow the farmer to sell his conserved water to the highest bidder. A water bank has been proposed in California and Utah which would permit potential buyers to make an offering and, depending on price, allow the farmer to decide whether to use or sell all or part of his water that year.

IV. THE CENTRAL ARIZONA PROJECT

9. The Wreck-lamation of America

We have seen that most of the claims for the necessity of additional water in the West are unjustified. Existent supplies of both surface and ground water are much more adequate than is claimed by the advocates of more water projects. With conservation and the use of waste water and especially the implementation of a more rational agriculture appropriate to the desert, the "need" for most, if not all, new water projects could be eliminated.

The Central Arizona Project is the largest and most expensive project under construction. We will examine it in detail. But first we must look at the part of the U.S. government that is most responsible—in cooperation with pork-barrelling politicians and other vested interests—for building it and other monstrously wasteful projects, the Bureau of Reclamation, called by some the Bureau of Wrecklamation.

It all began with the 1824 decision by the U.S. Supreme Court Chief Justice Marshall that the commerce clause of the Constitution gave the Federal Government the power to maintain all forms of transportation among the states. Congress immediately appropriated money for river improvements, which were primarily waterway developments. Financing other purposes, such as flood control, was understood to be unconstitutional. How the government arrived at today's world of big dams and big irrigation projects and

big subsidies is too long a story to tell in detail, but homesteading as a principal factor must be mentioned.

Homesteading was the major tool used to develop the
public lands and in the arid West, and irrigation was the
best way to produce crops. By 1899 the irrigation of private
lands amounted to 7.5 million acres. Advocates of direct
federal support for irrigation believed that private development of the public lands could not continue to grow after
1900 because the land that was inexpensive to develop would
soon be exhausted.

In the 1900 presidential campaign, all three political par-
ties favored irrigating lands in the West to stimulate the
homesteading of public lands, and in 1902 the Reclamation
Act was passed. The purpose of the act was summed up by
the first Reclamation Director:

. . . the object of the reclamation law is primarily to put the public
domain into the hands of small land owners—men who live upon
the land, support themselves, make prosperous homes, and become purchasers of the goods manufactured in the East and cotton
raised in the South.

Surely no one foresaw the use of this law to move the raising
of cotton from the South to the West.

Originally the money to construct projects to irrigate
lands came from a reclamation fund financed by sales of
public lands. By 1917 the Reclamation Service had 25 projects under its wing, enough to irrigate 1.8 million acres. By
the 1920s most of the best land had been homsteaded, so
little of the reclamation fund came from land reclaimed.
Today the big water projects of the West, built by the U.S.
Bureau of Reclamation, are funded by federal tax dollars,
either directly or indirectly.

The concept behind the building of these projects is that
the taxpayers put up the money, and the goods produced
by the finished project repay the taxpayers' loan. In its
August 1981 report to the Congress, the General Accounting
Office (GAO), which is known as the Congressional watch-
dog, reported that bureau reservoirs had 12 million acre
feet (af) of unsold water available for use. After 27 years of
operation, one reservoir built by the bureau has recovered
only 4% of the reimbursable cost. Not to be outdone, the

Army Corps of Engineers has been able to sell only 40,000 af of the 1,500,000 af available in their Williamette River Basin Project. GAO has concluded that it will take 1,500 years to repay the U.S. taxpayer. Yet both bureaucracies keep building more water projects.

Section 4 of the 10-section 1902 act deals with repayment of the costs of building irrigation projects: ". . . charges shall be determined with a view of returning to the reclamation fund the estimated cost of construction of the project. . . ." This was interpreted to mean that the irrigators were obligated to repay just the construction costs, not costs plus interest. Even with this subsidy, Congress had to several times extend repayment periods and in 1926 wrote off 13% of the costs of the original projects.

The fairness of using everyone's tax money to subsidize the few is every bit as questionable as using federal funds to move agriculture from the East to the West. By 1979 the Bureau of Reclamation projects were delivering the total water supply to approximately 11% of the irrigated acreage in the 17 western States and a supplemental supply to about 9%. The Corps of Engineers, Bureau of Indian Affairs, and Bureau of Land Management also have been involved in various phases of western irrigation development. These subsidized water projects obviously provide unfair competition to other western irrigators and to virtually every farmer in the nation. At the beginning of 1984 the federal government was attempting to foreclose on mortgages held by 250,000 farmers across the nation. As Dr. Thomas Power pointed out in his 1978 study, *An Economic Analysis of the Central Arizona Project, U.S. Bureau of Reclamation*: ". . . subsidized increases in supply can only be at the expense of farmers elsewhere and the taxpayer who supports farm incomes."

The agricultural surpluses of the 1920s led some to question the inconsistency of restricting production while subsidizing new farms in the West. It was pointed out that the interest-free loans, which reclamation policy essentially provided, gave irrigation farmers a large subsidy denied farmers elsewhere and created a special-interest group. These attacks continued into the 1930s, when the commissioner of the Bureau of Reclamation organized the National Reclamation Association, which "educated" Congress about the need to continue the subsidies. "Never were opponents of reclamation able to develop as strong a sectional vote in opposition as its advocates generally marshalled," according to Gates in his *History of Public Land Law Development.*

Our nation has been so blessed with agricultural surpluses that we have been paying farmers not to grow crops. At the same time, the bureau has been spending hundreds of millions of dollars to build water projects to continue the growth of these same crops. This absurd situation is succinctly summarized by Dr. Power in his 1978 economic analysis of the Central Arizona Project:

One hand of the government . . . is reducing while another, the BR, is doing the opposite, expanding agricultural output. . . . The BR and the Department of Agriculture are working at cross purposes making the citizen pay twice in increased taxes.

Proponents of reclamation were able to reduce repayment costs even further under a law passed in 1939. The Bureau of Reclamation interpreted the law as limiting the financial obligations of irrigation beneficiaries to their "ability to pay". In their 1981 analysis of six bureau projects under construction, the GAO found that the real value of the repayments was less than 8% of the cost to the Federal Government. This is significant since there were 32 bureau projects with irrigation facilities under construction in 1981, and their then-current cost estimate amounted to more than $14 billion. The CAP is by far the largest of these projects. Dr. Power's 1978 report calculated the capital gift to irrigators at $640 million, with an average of almost $2 million going to each 400-acre average farm. An acre is equivalent in size to a football field. It can hardly be argued that the owner of 400 football-field-sized farms with a guaranteed water supply is among the "truly needy" of our nation who should be subsidized by our taxes. In fact, such a farm would not have been eligible for reclamation subsidies under the original Reclamation Act.

Congressman Newlands, author of the 1902 Act, felt that 80 acres of irrigable land was all that should be permitted entrymen. As passed, the act prohibited the use of reclama-

tion water on lands "exceeding 160 acres to any one landowner" who must be "an actual bona fide resident on such
land." Congressman Newlands explained the purpose of
this section as follows:

The aim . . . is to prevent monopoly of every form, to open up
the public domain to actual settlers who desire homes, and to
disintegrate the monopolistic holdings of land that prevails on
the Pacific Coast and in the intermountain region.

This "160-acre limitation" was summarized in 1950 by
the President's Water Resources Policy Commission:

The acreage limitation has been construed, however, to permit
320 acres to be held jointly by husband and wife. Moreover, the
law does not preclude combined farming endeavor by any number
of owners, members of a family or otherwise, so long as each owns
no more than the acreage limit for any one owner.

What the law does not preclude, human nature will include, so by 1980 more than 60% of the acreage under
reclamation irrigation exceeded 320 acres. During this
period, the number of irrigated farms drastically declined,
even though the irrigated acreage continued to increase.

The bureau's 1980 "Interim Report on Acreage Limitation" shows that 48% of reclamation land is controlled by

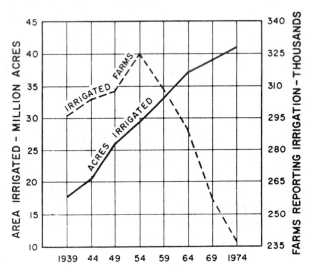

Fig. 26 The decline of the small irrigated farm. *U.S. Census of
Agriculture.*

9% of the landowners. Three hundred and forty-four owners individually own more than 1,280 acres. Their average holding is 2,752 acres. Obviously the Bureau of Reclamation was not enforcing the 160-acre provision.

In the late 1970s a California group called National Land for People sued the bureau, contending that lands in excess of the limitation should be sold so members of the group could purchase them and become small farmers. The courts agreed and directed the bureau to comply with the law. Almost immediately, powerful lobbies began pressuring Congress to repeal the restrictions. They based much of their case on the myth that farms must be large to be economically feasible.

The bureau's study shows that a farmer achieves most of the potential economies of size with 320 to 660 acres, depending on the type of farming. The study recognized that perennial crops like citrus, grapes, and apples required a much smaller acreage (under 100 acres) than field crops and vegetables or forage crops and cereals.

A 1967 study by the U.S. Department of Agriculture found that maximum efficiency occurs at a relatively small size and remains more or less constant through the very large range. The author of the study concluded that economies of scale were already present in the existing fully mechanized one- and two-man operations. A 1973 study by the USDA found the efficient size for a one-man farm in California was in the 200- to 400-acre range, and a 1981 study by the same agency noted that 90% efficiency could be attained by 300 acre farms in the corn belt and 232 acres in the wheat belt.

Yet we constantly hear that 1000-acre farms are needed for maximum efficiency. This may be true on the plains where dry farming prevails and there is substantially less rainfall than in the East. This was recognized as far back as the 1860s when it was questioned whether the 160-acre homestead was suited to the dryer portions of the Great Plains, and settlers were permitted to gain ownership of 320 acres. While the far west generally has even less rainfall, federal irrigation projects provide a more dependable water supply than is present in the humid east, where farms average 200 to 400 acres. The average size of a farm in a successful irrigation district near Tucson is 250 acres.

Congress either bought the bigger-is-better argument or responded to the lobbying efforts of the large landholders. It amended the Reclamation Act late in 1982. The "limitation" was raised to 960 acres. Our tax dollars are now being used to subsidize the owners of one and a half square miles of good farmland!

Congress chose to ignore the findings of the National Water Commission, which it authorized and funded with millions of dollars in 1968. The commission's 1973 report, "Water Policies for the Future," stated:

. . . No longer is it a national goal to stimulate settlement of the West. That goal has been accomplished; . . . Thus a principal basis for policies of providing free land and cheap irrigation water for Western farmers has disappeared . . .

Congress also ignored the March 1982 study by the U.S. General Accounting Office, which stated:

Our second observation is that the large subsidy given to irrigators is based on goals of homebuilding and settling the West. These goals were established at the beginning of the 20th century and were considered important enough for the Federal Government to step into what had been primarily private enterprise. The original rationale for subsidized irrigation projects is probably no longer applicable.

In their 1982 analysis, the economists from the University of Utah summarized the efforts of the Bureau of Reclamation to date: ". . . post-World War II operations of the Bureau certainly have failed to serve a modern interpretation of the bureau's equity and efficiency mandates (and quite possibly an historic one as well.)"

We have seen that the water crisis is centered in the bureau's bailiwick—the arid west, where 90% of the nation's irrigated land is located. Much of this can be attributed to government subsidies, and it can be argued that the water crisis has been created by government policies. The Central Arizona Project is the largest of all current bureau projects designed to alleviate the "crisis." It is much more the problem than the solution.

10. More Water at Any Price?

The Central Arizona Project is not needed to support human life since, as we have seen, the water already available to central Arizona is more than adequate. And the project is hardly an economic necessity. A large portion of its water would presumably go to Arizona agriculture, which consumes 89% of Arizona's present water supply but contributes only 2% to the state's personal income. What is this superfluous project and how did it come to be?

Soon after Arizona became a state in 1912, residents began promoting a plan to bring Colorado River water to central Arizona. In 1921 the chief engineer for the federal Reclamation Service called the concept a "Mad Man's Dream," but by 1947 that same agency, which had by then changed its name to the U.S. Bureau of Reclamation, completed a feasibility report which stated:

Unless additional irrigation water is made available to the project area, the equivalent of a 30% reduction in the presently cultivated lands in the area must eventually be effected. The Central Arizona Project is needed to sustain the agricultural economy of the area.

At that time Arizona farmed around 800,000 acres. Since 1951 the state's acreage has exceeded 1.1 million — an *increase* of more than 30%. In 1981 it exceeded 1.35 million acres.

With the solid support of every Arizona politician, the project was finally authorized in 1968. It consisted of 300 miles of aqueduct, 547,000 kilowatts of energy from the

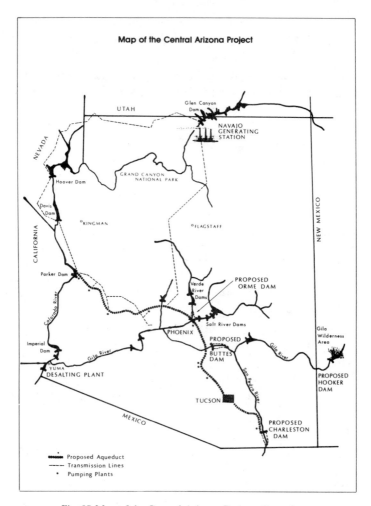

Fig. 27 Map of the Central Arizona Project. *Power Report.*

Navajo Power Plant in northern Arizona, and four dams
(see Figure 27). The major portion of the canal is deeper
than a two-story house and as wide as an eight-lane highway.
By 1983 the estimated construction cost was $3.5 billion,
the Navajo Power Plant was completed, and one-quarter of
the actual water delivery system had been funded. The
estimated completion date is sometime in the early 1990s,
which is important since Arizona need not repay the project
until it is "substantially completed."

Shortly before authorization, the solidarity of Arizona's support was shattered by several agricultural economists from the University of Arizona who pointed out that agriculture returned less than 10% to the state's personal income while consuming 90% of its water. More water was obviously a poor investment. From that point on, the project's purpose seemed to shift to a need for "water for survival" of Arizona's rapidly growing cities.

As we have seen, the facts belie the avowed justification of the project. But facts were in short supply in the early days of the CAP. Indeed, many Arizonans thought the CAP was the Civil Air Patrol! In Washington, Arizona was seen as a sand dune desert where people were dying of thirst. Most Arizonans assumed the project would be paid for by the federal government, while Congress was led to believe the CAP "loan" would be repaid by Arizona. Supporters of the project are eager to promote the myth that the CAP loan will not unduly tax Arizona or the nation.

In its 1977 review of the CAP, the U.S. Department of the Interior noted that the U.S. taxpayers will actually subsidize "at least 60%" of the CAP. While much of the *capital* cost of the project will be repaid by Arizona, irrigation recipients pay no interest on their portion of the federal loan. Municipal and industrial water recipients repay this 50 year loan at the rate of only 3.342%. It is unfortunate that the average American can't get such a deal when buying a home.

To understand the immensity of this subsidy, the analogy of a 50-year mortgage is helpful. At the 3% interest rate, the financing charge is equal to the capital cost of the home. At 6% the price of the home triples. With mortgage and other interest rates exceeding 12% in the early 1980s, the U.S. taxpayer is providing a massive subsidy to Arizona.

In his 1978 *An Economic Analysis of the Central Arizona Project*, Dr. Thomas Power, chairman of the economic department at the University of Montana, calculated the resulting federal subsidy to be $1.7 billion (in 1977 dollars) when compared with a 7% interest rate. He adds that "the subsidy from the U.S. taxpayer is likely to be significantly higher than calculated." The $1.7 billion estimated capital cost of the CAP at that time has since more than doubled.

Dr. Power also observed that the "CAP will cost Arizonans a terrific amount of money." His study shows that it will cost the state $1.4 billion in 1977 dollars. This is more than the entire state budget for that year. In 1980 dollars, it will cost more than $70 million a year just to operate the CAP. Arizonans will repay the CAP through increased property taxes and increased water rates.

In Arizona the unit of water measurement is the acre foot (af), which appears to be a uniquely Western concept, used to deal with large quantities of water. It is equal to 325,851 gallons. In 1980 the Salt River Project delivered water to the land in the Phoenix area for less than $7/acre foot. An acre is roughly equivalent in size to a football field, so an acre foot would cover that field with water one foot deep. A foot of dirt over the same area would cost more than $4,000, so water in the Phoenix area is not just "dirt cheap"—it is cheaper than dirt. The reason, of course, is that this water is highly subsidized. Even in its lowest value uses, it is worth twice its price. Numerous studies have calculated that the actual value of "new" water is around $15/af.

In its 1974 CAP report, Tucson noted that it was paying $20/af to pump groundwater and that CAP water would cost the city $135/af. In its 1977 review of the CAP, the U.S. Department of Interior confirmed the Tucson analysis when it noted that it would cost the U.S. Government $141/af to provide CAP water. Why would Arizona and the U.S. want to pay such an exorbitant amount for water when ample supplies are already available at a fraction of the cost? Perhaps Congress believes that in some way the benefits of the CAP justify the expenditures, but this is not true.

Before Congress authorizes a water project, it generally requires that the benefits produced will at least equal the cost of building. The Bureau of Reclamation's economic analysis of the CAP showed it would return $1.60 in benefits for each dollar invested. However, the bureau's parent agency, the Department of the Interior, severely criticized the bureau's economic analysis when it reviewed the CAP in 1977, and concluded that the CAP would return only 93 cents in benefits for each dollar invested at the 3.25% discount rate which was in effect when the project was authorized in 1968. Dr. Power provides a simplified explanation of the discount rate:

No one would pay a dollar today for an offer of a dollar 50 years from now. They would have to be offered a sum of money quite a bit larger than one dollar before they would agree to give up control and use of a dollar for fifty years. The discount rate is used to make this adjustment, to establish the equivalency between benefits in the future and their present worth.

The discount rate is *not* just an interest rate. It is a measure of what productive uses of resources in the private economy are lost as a result of the federal government taking the resources needed for CAP from private individuals and employing these resources in Arizona.

Since it seems unlikely that we will see 3.25% money again, the Interior Department analyzed the CAP at the 6.375% rate used in 1977 and found that with this figure there would be a return of only 58 cents in benefits for each dollar invested. It added that this "may still be overestimated in some respects."

Dr. Power's 1978 study found that the discount rate really averaged more than 11% but analyzed the CAP at the then "official government" rate of 7%. He concluded that at this latter rate, less than 35 cents in benefits would be realized on each dollar invested. The results of Dr. Power's analysis are shown in the appendix. In comparison Dr. Power also analyzed the bureau's Garrison Diversion Project in North Dakota and found its benefit-cost ration was less than one. His review of the bureau's O'Neil Project in Nebraska refers to an analysis by University of Nebraska agricultural economists, which estimated the benefit-cost ratio at 0.1 to 1. Dr. Power added: "This implies mere cents returned on each dollar invested."

In his review of the Oahe Unit in South Dakota, Dr. Power referred to a 1960 study which surveyed 43 existing irrigation projects and found that in only one-fourth of them did the benefits outweigh the costs. This knowledge was then applied to 30 proposed projects, and only one was found to have benefits in excess of costs. In summation, Dr. Power then observed: "That's the reason the Bureau of

Reclamation doesn't in general use the results of actual irrigation projects to produce the projections of what the benefits are going to be on new irrigation projects."

Again ignoring reality, the Bureau of Reclamation concluded that the value of CAP water to municipal and industrial (M&I) users was $200 an acre foot. This certainly is suspect, especially when water in the Phoenix area at that time was being sold for less than $7/af. How did the bureau arrive at a value for new CAP water that was almost 30 times the price of existing supplies, which are more than adequate for projected M&I growth? The bureau simply "assumed" that central Arizona cities would build their own CAP. Dr. Power in his 1978 study explains the meaning of this assumption:

Since the privately built unit would not be able to get capital from the government at a subsidized 3.25 percent but would have to borrow the money at market rates . . . the costs . . . are guaranteed to be higher. Thus no matter what the rationality of the M&I portion, no matter whether the water is needed or not, a higher positive benefit can be calculated by the BR.

The bureau's economic analysis also exaggerated agricultural benefits. It took as benefits the income that would be produced by using CAP water on new farms with the typical mix of cotton, grain, vegetables, etc. This is irrational because the CAP law specifically prohibits irrigating new farms. Also, classic economic theory would hold that CAP water would be used to grow low value crops, like alfalfa. Otherwise farms growing alfalfa with present supplies would instead be growing more valuable crops. While we have seen the value of additional water is only $15/af, the bureau managed to inflate the value of agricultural CAP water to $100/af. Since this is more than the cost of pumping groundwater, there would be no benefits to farms that rely on that source.

The Department of the Interior summarized its criticism of the bureau's economic analysis as follows:

These problems reflect a general failure on the part of the Bureau of Reclamation in its benefit-cost analysis for the Central Arizona Project to make a serious attempt to determine what would happen in central Arizona without the Central Arizona Project and then to compare this with what would happen if the Central Arizona Project is built.

We have already determined what would happen in central Arizona without the CAP. There is ample renewable water for cities and industries and enough groundwater to permit most farms to remain in business for well over a century. Of course, the depths to groundwater would continue to increase. The benefits from CAP water could be calculated as the difference between the cost of pumping groundwater and the cost of CAP water. The Department of the Interior concluded that the depth to groundwater would have to exceed 1000 feet to justify the cost of CAP water. They added that the present depth to groundwater generally ranges from 300 to 500 feet.

Simple logic could be substituted for all this economic analysis. The energy required to pump water *up* from underground is same as pumping water *up*hill from the Colorado River. CAP water will be pumped uphill 1200 feet to Phoenix and another 900 feet to Tucson. Therefore the groundwater depths would have to exceed 1200 feet to justify pumping CAP water uphill to Phoenix and exceed 2100 feet to pump to Tucson. Then the cost of building the CAP would have to be added.

The CAP will consume 547,000 kilowatts of energy to lift water uphill into central Arizona. As hard as it is to believe, the bureau used this consumption of precious energy as a benefit! Again quoting Dr. Power:

This magic which transforms a major electric cost into a major electric benefit is possible because lumped in with CAP is an electric generating facility which already exists and which has nothing to do with the CAP.

This energy is provided by the Navajo Power plant which produces $2.25 in benefits for each dollar invested. Including the power plant with CAP was simply a ploy to make CAP look better. It has no economic logic, as Dr. Power points out.

Diverting the funds of the Navajo plant to CAP is no different than diverting tax revenues to CAP. Both remove monies from the federal treasury. Yet, hopefully, no one would claim federal tax revenues as a benefit of CAP.

The Navajo Plant provides yet another benefit to the bureau—it permits the claim that a greater portion of the CAP is completed than is in fact true, thus making the public believe it is too late to reconsider the project. As of June 1981, the bureau claimed that it was one-third complete. However 30% of the money spent was for the power plant. Less than one-quarter of the CAP was funded at that time.

The high price of CAP water does not bother some, who contend it will produce thousands of jobs. There is no doubt that during the construction period, the project will do just that. The more important question is whether investing in this type of project is the best way to employ people.

A 1983 Congressional Budget Office study noted that "Water projects are not the most efficient investments to stimulate jobs or countercyclical economic development." The Bureau of Reclamation and the Corps of Engineers are the major builders of water projects. This type of construction creates relatively few jobs because it is highly mechanized. In addition the workers are generally transient, so unemployment in the project areas remains unaffected.

A 1973 study in the *American Society of Civil Engineers Journal* reported that 30% more jobs could be created by shifting investments from Corps of Engineers construction projects to waste treatment plant construction. One of the authors reaffirmed his findings in testimony before the U.S. Congress on the 1983 "Jobs" bill. He was ignored as Congress appropriated hundreds of millions of dollars for bureau and corps projects, including $15 million for the CAP. More than $50,000 is required to create each job provided by Bureau of Reclamation projects. An attempt to transfer $200 million to wastewater treatment was thwarted, even though it would help curb pollution while providing 30% more jobs.

The 1973 study also noted that tax relief would provide 11% more jobs by allowing the individual consumer to spend the money. Therefore from an employment standpoint it would be far better to reduce spending on water projects like the CAP.

Former Secretary of the Interior Cecil Andrus was aware of most of these facts when he told President Carter in a

February 14, 1977, memo:

Because of its scope, expense, and environmental degradation we have identified the CAP as one of the least meritorious of the Bureau of Reclamation projects (albeit with strong local political support).

In spite of this, President Carter bowed to congressional pressure and reinstated the Central Arizona Project.

11. The Last Waterhole

The Central Arizona Project is to be supplied by water from the Colorado River. It is indeed fortunate that central Arizona has an adequate water supply because many analysts are convinced that this river, Arizona's "last waterhole," will soon be dry.

The Colorado River originates in the ski country of Colorado, where it is fed by the melting snow and cascading streams of the high Rockies. Almost from its source, part of its waters are diverted through the mountains to Denver, while the remainder flows across the southeast corner of Utah and into Arizona. Tributaries such as the Green and San Juan rivers supplement its flow. The states from which the rivers originated and through which they flow form the "Upper Basin" states: Colorado, Wyoming, Utah and New Mexico. After its release from Glen Canyon Dam, the river enters the Grand Canyon and flows through the arid "Lower Basin" states of Arizona, Nevada, and California. After major diversions in the latter, it enters Mexico where its last drop of water is drained before it has a chance to flow into the Gulf of California.

In 1922 these seven states of the Colorado River Basin joined in a compact to apportion the waters of the great river. Its flow had exceeded 20 million acre feet (maf) on six occasions and in 1917 reached 24 maf. Therefore the states felt comfortable dividing 15 maf between the Upper and Lower Basins. In 1934 the United States entered into

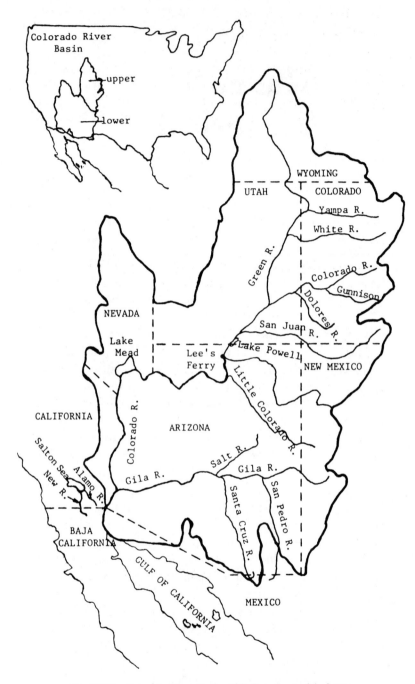

Fig. 28 The Colorado River Basin. *U.S. Department of the Interior.*

a treaty which gave Mexico an additional 1.5 maf, making the total apportioned 16.5 maf.

But as Table 5, from a 1977 National Academy of Science study shows, though 1896 through 1929 was a "wet period" for the river, its flow averaged only 16.8 maf, which barely satisfies the amount apportioned. The years 1930 to 1968, on the other hand, was a "dry period" with an annual flow of only 13.0 maf. The important question is therefore, which period is truly representative of the river's flow? The Bureau of Reclamation insists upon using the average flow of the entire 73-year period to show that there is 14.8 maf available—but even that is insufficient for the apportionment. The Upper Colorado River Commission officials accept 13.7

Table 5: Colorado River at Lee Ferry, Arizona, Estimated Average Annual Virgin Flow*

Period	Average Annual Virgin-Flow (million acre feet)	Remarks
1896-1968	14.8	73-year period of measured flow and estimates by federal agencies
1896-1929	16.8	34-year "wet period"
1930-1968	13.0	38-year "dry period"
1922-1966	13.8	45-year period of measured flow
1914-1923	18.8	10-year wettest period
1931-1940	11.8	10-year driest period
Total Flow		
1917	24.0	Maximum single year
1934	5.6	Minimum single year

*Quantities are for water years October 1 - September 30, inclusive. Gauging station established in 1921. Prior to 1922 estimates are based on measurements at upstream stations. (Colorado River Board of California. 1969) maf as more reliable, and engineers for the Lower Basin testified during the 1968 CAP hearings that the flow is between 13.7 and 14 maf per year. A 1971 analysis by Resources for the Future, Inc. placed the dependable supply at only 12.7 maf.

The study of tree rings from living trees or wood from archaeological sites can indicate wet and dry years over a period of centuries. The flow of rivers can be inferred from this data. In 1975 the University of Arizona completed a tree ring analysis which shows that the flow in the Colorado Basin in the early part of this century was abnormally high. In fact, the last time such high flows occurred was in the early 1600s. The study concluded that the average yearly flow of the river is 13.5 maf.

The U.S. General Accounting Office (GAO) in its May 1979 report on Colorado River Basin water problems summed up the tree ring research as follows:

The tree ring studies show that the period 1930 to 1977 is a normal period when viewed in the context of the past few centuries. Using the Bureau's historical data for this period, the average virgin flow was 13.2 maf.

The second chapter of this report is entitled, "Water Supply is Insufficiant to Meet Future Demands." It begins with the following summary:

Most authorities agree there will be a future water shortage in the basin. The question is when and how bad. Many feel that the basin as a whole will experience a surface water shortage sometime after the year 2000. Others say it will occur sooner and be more severe than projected by the Bureau of Reclamation.

According to this GAO report, even the Bureau of Reclamation admits the shortage could occur as early as 1992.

When the shortage occurs will be determined by the water use of the Upper Basin states, which is the subject of our next chapter. For our discussion here, the important point is that the apportionment compact requires the Upper Basin to release 7.5 maf to the Lower Basin. The Lower Basin states has apportioned 4.4 maf of this for California, .3 maf for Nevada and 2.8 maf for Arizona (1 maf of this is for the CAP). However, most analysts believe that half of the

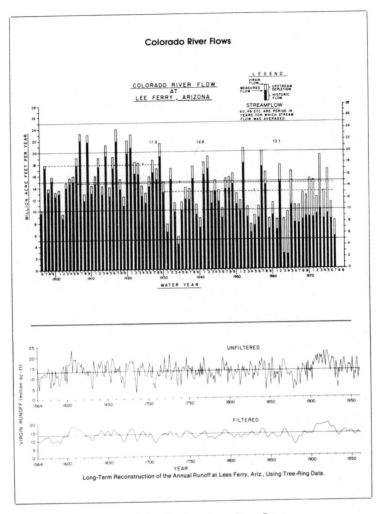

Fig. 29 Colorado River flows. *Power Report.*

Mexican commitment must be provided by the Lower Basin and that this .75 maf comes off the top since international treaties would seem to take priority over agreements between states.

For some reason no one included Lower Basin evaporation losses in the apportionment, and even the bureau estimates nets losses at .7 maf. The impartial U.S. Geological Survey estimates net losses at 1.3 maf (Lake Mead alone evaporates .8 maf). Adding a conservative .85 maf for net losses to the .75 maf for Mexico leaves only 5.9 maf available for Lower Basin consumption. In recent years, California alone has been consuming 5 maf, and Nevada has developed its .3 maf. Arizona's perfected rights along the River amount to 1.2 maf. This is possible only because the Upper Basin has not developed its allocation, as we will discuss later.

In the 1963 dispute between Arizona and California, the Special Master decided that the reduced amount should be shared on a pro rata basis. California, therefore, would receive the same proportion of the 5.9 maf as it would have received of the originally projected 7.5 maf. This would amount to 3.4 maf (4.4/7.5 × 5.9 = 3.4). The Supreme Court agreed that this method seemed "equitable on its face. . . ." but added that the choice among recognized methods is up to the Secretary of Interior.

In 1968, the method was determined—to the detriment of Arizona. To get California's vote for the CAP, Arizona had to ignore the recommended pro rata sharing plan and guarantee California the first 4.4 maf coming down the river. Table 6 compares the result of this agreement with the results of the pro rata method that might have been used before the 1968 CAP law was enacted. The implication is clear: Arizona may have given up one million acre feet of water (which could have been used in any way the state wished) forever in order to be able to bring the same amount to central Arizona for what may be a very few years and at a cost of well over a billion dollars.

Table 6: Colorado River Allocations

	Before CAP	After CAP
Compact release	7.5	7.5
Mexican treaty	-.75	-.75
Lower Basin losses	-.85	-.85
Lower Basin supply	5.9	5.9
California	-3.4	-4.4
Arizona & Nevada —existing use	-1.5	-1.5
Available for CAP	1.0	0.0

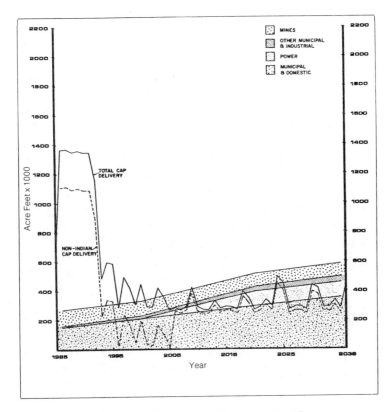

Fig. 30 Colorado River dependable supply. *Power Report.*

Arizona's Senator Carl Hayden apparently recognized this and tried to limit California's guarantee to 1994, but California would not vote for the CAP without making the term perpetual. Small wonder that California continually supports the CAP. In fact, California's support might be the biggest obstacle Arizonans will have to confront should they decide to stop the CAP. On the other hand, California will lose the water it has been using in excess of 4.4 maf if CAP is built. California used this argument in the early 1980s in an effort to get funding approved by its voters to import more water from the north.

Proponents of the CAP point out that the storage capacity of the reservoirs on the Colorado is 60 maf, enough to supply the CAP through its 50-year economic life. But while still claiming that the CAP supply will "average" a little more than 1.0 maf a year, the Bureau of Reclamation admits that the amount will not be available each year. In fact, their "dependable supply" is rather disheartening. The maximum supply is available for less than 10 years, then drastically decreases while the demand continues to increase.

Opponents point out that the reservoirs may not be filled to capacity when the CAP goes on line, adding that the river's flow was only 8 maf in 1981. They also note that even if the reservoirs are full, only half their storage can be depleted before their hydroelectric power production is severely curtailed. Finally, they point out that only half the reservoir storage is in the Lower Basin. The other half is in the Upper Basin which is not likely to cooperate when there is not enough water in the Colorado River for all competing interests.

12. More Pork Barrel Projects

Sooner or later the Central Arizona Project will be looking for water, as our discussion has indicated, and the project's completion will be the prime catalyst in a chain reaction. Secretary of the Interior Andrus summed up the situation in a February 14, 1977, memo to President Carter:

There is a significant inter-relationship between the Central Arizona Project and a number of questionable projects in the state of Colorado. Authorization of Savery Pot-Hook, Dolores, Fruitland Mesa and several other uneconomic Colorado projects was the political trade-off extracted by then House Interior Committee Chairman Wayne Aspinall for authorizing the CAP . . . Thus, if funding is deleted for the CAP, there is no reason whatsoever to pursue the Upper Basin projects in Colorado. But, if the CAP is continued, pressure will persist to fulfill the Upper Basin part of the "bargain."

Here is a description of "Pork Barrel" politics—the trade-offs made by various congressmen to get their pet projects built. The economic burden on the national taxpayer was irrelevant, as is amply illustrated by two of the projects mentioned. Fruitland Mesa and Savery Pot-Hook would return benefits of only 30 cents for each federal dollar invested. President Carter, to his credit, cut further funding for these two projects, but the political furor created by his "hit list" forced him to back down on other "uneconomic" projects.

Dolores is one of the five projects included in the 1968 CAP legislation in order to get the votes of the Upper Basin congressmen. It is located in southwestern Colorado on the Dolores River, just northwest of Mesa Verde National Park. It includes several dams, pumping plants, and canals. When authorized, its cost was $54 million but by 1981 this had risen to $298 million. The Carter Review Team found it would return only 60 cents in benefits for each dollar invested. President Carter did not recommend abandoning it, and it has continued to receive appropriations.

Another of these five projects under construction is Dallas Creek. It is also on the western slope of Colorado's Rocky Mountains, in the vicinity of Montrose. Authorized at $38 million in 1968, President Carter's review team calculated its benefit/cost ratio at .9/1.0, but again the administration did not abandon its construction. Both projects will have salinity impacts on the Colorado River, resulting in additional impacts on the taxpaying public.

As of 1983 Colorado continued to seek appropriations for the construction of a third CAP related water project in the southwestern part of the state: the Animas—La Plata project. Originally authorized at $116 million, its estimated cost had risen to $520 million by 1982.

So much for the pork barrel projects that Colorado garnered for its vote authorizing the CAP. As already noted, California received its guaranteed supply provision. New Mexico was awarded Hooker Dam on its southwest border with Arizona, which is particularly controversial because it would inundate portions of the first wilderness area established by Congress. Utah was scheduled to get money for the Dixie Project in the southern part of that state.

This array of trade-offs seems insignificant compared to another Utah project, however—the Central Utah Project. The CUP's cost is well over a billion dollars. By far the largest portion of it is the Bonneville Unit, which consists of 10 reservoirs and 140 miles of aqueduct, tunnels and canals. Powers shows that it will return less than 32 cents in benefits for every federal tax dollar spent. Thus the CUP's initials are not the only similarity to the CAP. Comments made in a letter from R. Paul Van Dam, Salt Lake County Attorney, to the Board of County Commissioners on July 5, 1977, would lead one to conclude that Salt Lake City's water problems are not dissimilar to those in the Phoenix area:

... In short, we have enough water for many years to come without Bonneville Unit water i[f] institutional barriers to water supplies are removed.

All these Upper Basin projects will be consuming the waters of the Colorado River, hastening the arrival of the "inevitable water crisis." In addition, there will be demands placed upon this already over-allocated river by the energy crisis. Vast quantities of coal lie in the Upper Basin of the Colorado River. Substantial oil shale deposits are also located there. In January 1980 the General Accounting Office issued a report entitled "Water Supply Should Not Be an Obstacle to Meeting Energy Development Goals." In 1981, Exxon stated that it hoped to produce 8 billion barrels of shale oil a day by the end of the century, primarily from Colorado and Wyoming deposits. They proposed piping water in from the Missouri River or the Gulf of Mexico, since there is not enough water in the Upper Basin to permit extraction of this amount of oil.

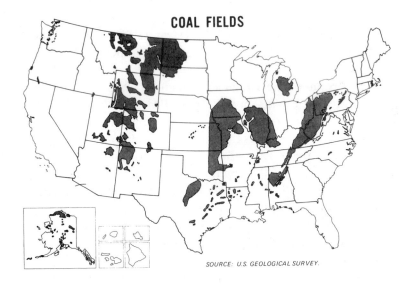

COAL FIELDS

SOURCE: U.S. GEOLOGICAL SURVEY.

Fig. 31 The nation's coal fields. *U.S. Geological Survey.*

Exxon subsequently backed off their massive project, because of the oil glut, but energy development in the West has only slowed, not stopped. In 1982 Ballard, Devine, et al. in *Water and Western Energy* stated:

In summary, water availability and quality problems in the West are already serious and are likely to become worse even without energy resource development. Although energy development is not the major cause of most water problems, it is likely to exacerbate many of them. Thus, energy development could be constrained in many areas of the West because of these conflicts . . .

This was followed in 1983 by the American Association of Engineering Societies' Energy Statement II, which noted: "One of the main differences in this statement and the one delivered in 1980 lies in the increased importance placed on coal and synthetic liquid derivatives to augment the nation's energy supply."

With this background, we can now look at the Upper Basin water picture. Most observers believe that the Upper Basin must release half of the Mexican commitment. This is contested by some in the Upper Basin, however. Added to the 7.5 maf discussed in the previous chapter, the total release to the Lower Basin becomes 8.25 maf. With the annual flow of the Colorado River at 13.5 maf, the Upper Basin states could consume only 5.25 maf under this scenario.

According to the 1974 Department of Interior's "Report on Water for Energy in the Upper Colorado River Basin," consumption by the Upper Basin could reach 5.25 maf before 1990. There seems little doubt, based upon this report, that this water crisis will develop before 2000. When the crisis occurs, the CAP, southern California, and the Upper Basin states will all be looking for water. Who will suffer the most is an important question.

Most observers in the Lower Basin believe that the Upper Basin must release 8.25 maf a year to the Lower Basin, but this has little basis in the "Law of the River." The latter consist primarily of the 1922 Colorado River Compact, the first interstate stream compact in the nation's history, as consented to by Congress with the 1928 Boulder Canyon

Act and affirmed by various court decisions. Article III (d) of the compact states:

The states of the Upper Division will not cause the flow of the river . . . to be depleted below an aggregate of 75,000,000 acre-feet for any period of ten consecutive years . . .

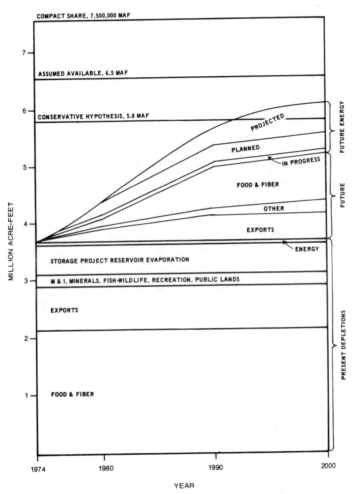

Fig. 32 Upper Basin projected water depletion. *U.S. Department of the Interior.*

Therefore the required release is not 7.5 maf a year but 75 maf over a period of 10 years. As for the Mexican commitment, Article III (c) says it shall be "equally borne by the Upper Basin and the Lower Basin," and that it shall be "in addition to"the 75 maf. To further complicate matters, Article III (a) says:

There is hereby apportioned from the Colorado River System in perpetuity to the Upper Basin and to the Lower Basin, respectively, the exclusive beneficial consumptive use of 7,500,000 acre-feet of water per annum, . . .

This opens a Pandora's Box of possibilities. It would appear that the Upper Basin could consume 7.5 maf while releasing only its share of the Mexican commitment. This would be particularly significant during drought years like 1981 where the River's flow was only 8 maf. As we saw in the last chapter, the lowest flow in the River was only 5.6 maf, and the 10-year driest period saw an average annual flow of only 11.8 maf. The fact that half of the Colorado River reservoir storage is in the Upper Basin is significant since theoretically they could make minimal releases for several years and then release large amounts from storage to satisfy the 75 maf per decade requirement.

The Director of the Colorado Water Conservation Board ended his 1976 *Synopsis* of events relating to the Colorado River by observing: "The final chapter in the continuing struggle over the waters of the Colorado River has not yet been written—and may never be." He noted that in the 1922 Compact, the Lower Basin's 7.5 maf included the Gila River Basin. This includes the Salt and Verde, with a total flow of approximately 1.5 maf. This of course would raise the annual flow from 13.5 maf to 15 maf, which would have permitted the Upper Basin to consume almost 7 maf instead of the 5.25 already discussed.

The Supreme Court of the United States in its 1963 Arizona vs. California decision did not include the Gila, however. This certainly seems questionable since the Upper Basin's Green, Gunnison, San Juan, and other tributary rivers were included in their apportionment. The Green River is every bit as long as the Gila. Since the Upper Basin states were not a party to the 1963 decision, it seems reasonable to conclude that they will be in court when the crisis comes. The resultant lawsuit between the Upper and Lower Basins would surely rival the 10-year battle between Arizona and California.

Anything is possible in this wonderful world of western water. In 1934 the governor of Arizona sent troops to prevent the construction of Parker Dam, the diversion point for the aqueduct which carries Colorado River water to California. With apportionments of 16.5 maf and a flow of only 13.5 maf, it doesn't seem possible for each basin to get 7.5 maf per year—unless more water is imported into the Colorado River Basin.

13. North to Alaska

Since we are not likely to build a multi-billion dollar water project without having water for it, Arizona will be looking for more water to fill the CAP. The state will undoubtedly be joined in that quest by California since the CAP takes away water that state is now using. It is probable that the Upper Basin states will join in the clamor for more water to form an increasingly powerful coalition. No doubt the Bureau of Reclamation will work closely with this group in order to get more projects to build.

There have been many proposals made to supplement the water supply of these western states. More than a dozen plans have been formulated since 1963. One of the more modest schemes would transport 2.4 maf a year from the Snake River in Idaho at a cost of $2.1 billion. Another would bring 15 maf annually from the Columbia River in Oregon but at a cost of $18.6 billion. Both estimates are in 1972 dollars.

Idaho, Washington, and Oregon have millions of acres of unused irrigable lands and are understandably reluctant to send their water to the other areas. Accordingly, they included a provision in the 1968 law authorizing the CAP that such importation studies would not be permitted for 10 years. This was renewed in 1978, but the growth and resultant political power of the southwest could prevent subsequent postponements.

The important point here is that additional states are seeking more water. The increasing depletion of the Ogallala Aquifer in the plains could add even more states to the growing list, setting the stage for the granddaddy of all water importation projects—the North American Water and Power Alliance (NAWAPA).

While the CAP was being discussed in Congress in the mid-'60s, this grandiose plan was being conceived by a California engineering and construction firm. It would bring water from Alaska and Canada to the western United States and northern Mexico. Primary storage would be facilitated by a 500-mile long reservoir in the Rocky Mountain Trench, adjacent to Banff and Jasper National Parks.

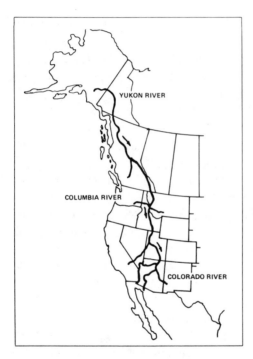

Fig. 33 North American Water and Power Alliance Plan. *Power Report.*

The 1974 "Conceptual Study" promotes NAWAPA in the same manner that the CAP and other water projects were promoted:

Water is now our number one continental problem and must be solved on a continental scale. Previously, water supply shortages were considered local problems to be solved by metropolitan areas or agricultural districts. . . . At present, Canada, the United States, and Mexico are experiencing tremendous increases in population. . . . This population growth is greatly accelerating the demand for water. . . . More water is required to sustain life, to produce the necessities of life, and to provide recreational facilities to absorb man's ever increasing leisure time. . . . What causes this ever-increasing demand for more and more water? More land is irrigated to produce food, fibers, and timber. More water is needed in our cities to support and protect increasing populations. . . .

We have already seen the fallacies of these arguments. Our cities have more than ample supplies for the future. Our agricultural surplus is the envy of the world. But the bandwagon is already rolling. In 1977 *Time* magazine credited Arizona Congressman John Rhodes, the House minority leader, with reviving the NAWAPA Plan. It noted that NAWAPA's cost could exceed $200 billion, almost one hundred times the cost of the CAP. Other national publications, such as the influential *Forbes* magazine, discussed NAWAPA at this time.

According to a January 16, 1982, *Arizona Republic* news article, NAWAPA's price had risen to $500 billion. The fact that this approaches the amount of the federal budget did not shock this conservative newspaper, possibly because the plan's promoters suggested that the CAP could be used to deliver 12 of the plan's 110 million acre feet to Arizona. This confirms a 1976 statement by promoters of the plan that NAWAPA "has always been considered as an augmenting feature of the Central Arizona Project . . ."

In early 1982 more than a dozen meetings were held in major cities throughout the West leading to a "National Conference on Water from Alaska" in Houston, Texas, on February 27, 1982. A spokesperson for the non-partisan National Democratic Policy Committee, which reportedly had 12,000 members, proposed in the same *Arizona Republic* newspaper article that a study of the plan should be funded through federal taxes since it is "an appropriate plan for national-economic redevelopment . . ." This reiterates the following quote from the 1974 conceptual study:

Previously, water supply shortages were considered local problems to be solved by metropolitan areas or agricultural districts . . . Within the past few years, however, it has become clear that water shortages cannot be solved locally . . . but must be attacked on a continental basis.

National-economic redevelopment is nothing new. In the West, it has been called reclamation. As we have seen, metropolitan water shortages in the areas that NAWAPA would serve can be solved locally by upgrading antiquated laws and policies.

Now we find that the water projects of the past and present will be dwarfed by those planned for the future. It is most frustrating when one realizes that NAWAPA would bring more water to the West while millions of acres of prime farmland are available in the East, where the same crops can be grown with "God Water," as one farmer has put it. It is obvious that the Bureau of Reclamation will be selected to build these massive, new western water projects.

The future could be even better without the federal government's assistance in the form of reclamation. Contrary to NAWAPA promotional propaganda, big-government is not the solution to water woes. Rather it is the changing of policy at the local level, as Dr. Kelso and his fellow agricultural economists at the University of Arizona stated so succinctly in their 1973 analysis of Arizona's water supply:

In sum, the Arizona water problem is more a problem of the lack of man-made institutions (policies) for developing and transferring water than a problem of physically short supplies. At least, the problem can be resolved more cheaply for many years to come if it is approached through institutional (policy) reform relating to water transfer rather than through development and/or importation of additional water supplies. The water problem in Arizona is a "man-problem" rather than a "nature-problem."

In America, the institution for developing and transferring commodities has traditionally been the free-market system. Unfortunately, as Dr. Kelso and his colleagues pointed out in one of their early papers, the western states have adopted a "Water is Different Syndrome." The University of Utah economists stated in their 1979 paper:

. . . Many economists would argue that heavier reliance on unsubsidized and unencumbered markets would yield more efficient resource allocations than either the old-style or new-style governmental planning . . .

V. MORE PROBLEMS AND SOME SOLUTIONS

14. Water Mining

Mining groundwater in Arizona was discussed earlier. The 1978 Second National Water Assessment by the U.S. Water Resources Council found many other areas in the nation which are removing water from underground storage faster than nature can replenish it. The largest area is in the heart of America's farmland, the Great Plains. Overlying the Ogallala Aquifer, it encompasses 225,000 square miles, including parts of the high plains of Oklahoma, Kansas, Texas, South Dakota, Nebraska, and Colorado.

This is the region of the infamous "dust bowl," where poor farming practices and severe drought destroyed the land in the 1930s. The land has been brought back to life

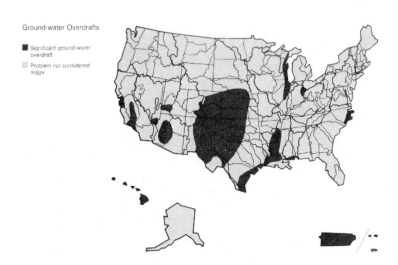

Ground-water Overdrafts

■ Significant ground-water overdraft

▨ Problem not considered major

Fig. 34 Groundwater mining in America. *U.S. Soil Conservation Service.*

through good conservation practices and, to a large extent, by mining the groundwater from the Ogallala Aquifer. Thirty-thousand of the area's 77,000 farms use some irrigation, accounting for almost a fifth of the nation's irrigated farmland.

Politicians and the news media are increasingly warning us that the aquifer will soon run out of water. Proposals have been made to import water from other areas, such as Arkansas and Missouri, with 1977 price tags ranging from $5 billion to $22 billion. Some plans require the pumping of water uphill more than 2,500 feet, even though all but one (Colorado) of six states, are already among the highest in the nation in energy consumption per irrigated acre. All the states are within the bailiwick of the Bureau of Reclamation.

Recharge to this aquifer is very small, amounting to less than one inch per year in the southern part, which is known as the Texas High Plains. Declines in the water level due to pumping are on the order of two to three feet per year. Experts predict the ultimate exhaustion of the aquifer, but it can be assumed that the relatively small communities, all of which are substantially less than 200,000 people, will have adequate water for the future.

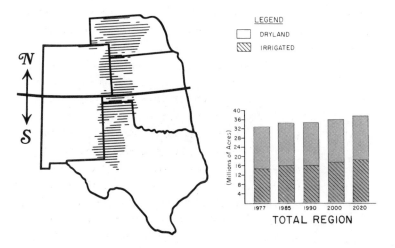

Fig. 35 The Ogallala aquifer. *U.S. Department of Commerce.*

The big question is, when will the area run out of water at the present rate of mining? In July 1982 two national engineering firms completed the *Six-State High Plains Ogallala Aquifer Regional Resources Study.* It indicated that the water supply within the aquifer would last for more than a century. Obviously there is no need to panic. The study also showed that the supplies under the southern part of the aquifer are substantially less copious, however, and could be depleted in 50 years or so. It also noted that "Some areas such as in the South High Plains of Texas are either out of water or water levels have dropped below economically feasible pumping lifts." Thus we are presented with the very real possibility that the increasingly high cost of energy might force irrigated agriculture out of business—just as it has driven many other businesses into bankruptcy. What would be the effect on the nation with this reduction in irrigated agriculture?

The major irrigated crops of the region are corn, wheat and sorghum. Approximately 2 million acres are in cotton, almost all of which are in Texas. These are the surplus crops and represent more than 10% of the acreage that was "set aside" in 1983. To build projects to rescue surplus crops makes even less sense than paying farmers not to grow surplus crops. This policy could result in a never-ending cycle, for as the 1973 National Water Commission study found: ". . . the dominant theme of the studies of American agriculture is overproduction accompanied by a depressed economy." If government policy is to reduce the mining of groundwater, however, and to continue to control over-production through set-aside payments, it could at least give priority to those acreages where water is being mined.

What happens if the government does nothing and the free market is permitted to function? Energy costs or deple-tions of portions of the aquifer would force an increasing number of farmers to switch from irrigation to the dryland farming which is presently employed by more than half the farmers in the area. This would result in decreased produc-tion, since irrigation with its guaranteed water supply is generally more productive than dryland farming. The major effect would be a reduction in the amount of surplus crops grown in the nation—and, of course, a reduction in the amount of groundwater mining.

Such a scenario coincides with the conclusion of the National Society of Professional Engineers' 1983 position paper on water policy: ". . . planning to offset production deline as groundwater sources are depleted should fully explore alternatives to increase dryland production . . ."

Switching from irrigation to dryland farming obviously will not work as well in the southwestern United States with its scant rainfall. To discuss this scenario, let us return to Arizona which has the second largest area of groundwater overdraft. While we painted with rather a broad brush in our discussion of the Great Plains, here we can be much more specific since we have already discussed the water resources in depth. What happens if energy costs or aquifer depletion causes farms to go out of business in Arizona?

First it should be noted that the high cost of pumping groundwater is more likely to cause a reduction in Arizona agriculture than is a lack of water stored underground. At the rate that Arizona has been mining its aquifers, the known quantities of water in storage under the state will last for more than 500 years. In central Arizona the present rate of overdrafting could also continue for centuries. However, Tucson has been purchasing farmlands in order to acquire their water rights, and Arizona's 1980 groundwater law provides the mechanism for purchasing and retiring farmlands. What can these displaced farmers do?

All too frequently Americans are displaced as the government uses its power of eminent domain to build highways, water projects, and even parks. Homeowners and business interests can relocate, but where do desert farmers go? They have lost their water rights, since these go with the land. In many cases they could retire on their profits. They could also remain in Arizona and continue farming, possibly without contributing to the overdraft of the aquifers.

There is plenty of unused irrigable land in Arizona. Most of this land is underlain by groundwater deposits. Farmers could relocate to these areas and use the untapped underground water resources there. Note that much of the irrigable land is near Arizona's western border. This is where

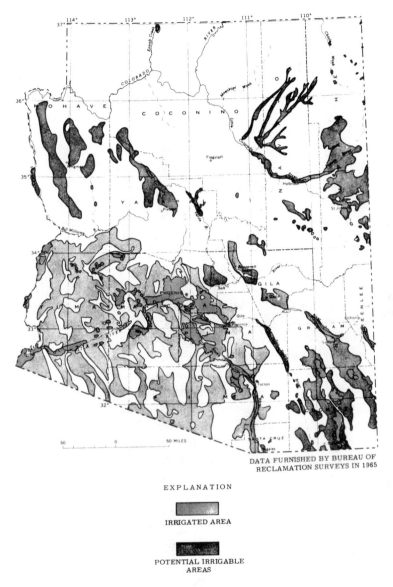

DATA FURNISHED BY BUREAU OF
RECLAMATION SURVEYS IN 1965

EXPLANATION

IRRIGATED AREA

POTENTIAL IRRIGABLE
AREAS

Fig. 36 Potential irrigable lands in Arizona. *Arizona Bureau of Mines.*

the Colorado River flows, and the state has unused rights
to enough water in that river to irrigate hundreds of
thousands of acres of land. Bureau of Reclamation studies
have shown that more than 500,000 acres could be irrigated

from the Colorado River in the Yuma area alone in the extreme southwest corner of the state.

Apparently heeding the "Go West, young man" advice popularized by Horace Greeley, there has been a 50% increase in farming in western Arizona through the decade of the '70s. The state could continue this trend by encouraging farmers in areas where groundwater is mined to relocate to the west to irrigate with the renewable water of the Colorado River. Some of the unused irrigable lands there are state school trust lands which the state could trade for land of equal value in overdrafted areas.

Most of the groundwater mining in Arizona occurs in the center of the state, and three-quarters of the irrigated acreage there consists of cotton and grain. These of course are the surplus crops that the federal government has been paying farmers not to grow. Again if the federal government feels it must subsidize agriculture, it could at least set aside the lands in central Arizona that are based on mining water and growing surplus crops.

The federal government seems to think it has a duty to solve Arizona's groundwater overdraft, since that is a major purpose of the multi-billion dollar Central Arizona Project. Rather than bringing Colorado River water to central Arizona, the government could encourage farmers to move to the river. Much of the land near the River is under the control of the Bureau of Land Management (BLM) and other federal agencies. The United States could trade some of these lands for those in central Arizona that are growing surplus crops and overdrafting.

This would provide a permanent solution at virtually no cost to the taxpayer. The "abandoned" land in central Arizona would have to be provided with a cover of native vegetation to prevent blowing dust and erosion, and the wells would have to be capped. For a slightly larger investment, these abandoned farmlands could help provide our nation with insurance against two of mankinds greatest fears, drought and famine. In the event of such catastrophes, these lands could quickly resume full production by maintaining the pumps and irrigation ditches. Essentially we would be "mothballing" our irrigated lands and their underground water supplies, just as we mothballed our warships after the Second World War.

This plan has other implications for Arizona's future. A 1975 study concluded that central Arizona could barely stand to double its population without severe disruption of its lifestyle. In 1976 Phoenix ranked in the top ten cities in the U.S. in terms of air pollution problems. Its air quality was poorer than Philadelphia, Baltimore, and Detroit.

One solution to pollution is dilution. Rather than continuing to concentrate growth in central Arizona, opening new lands in western Arizona could prevent increased pollution by dispersing the state's future population. One of Governor Babbitt's inaugural goals in 1978 was the dispersal of population to smaller communities. The Chambers of Commerce of such western Arizona communities as Yuma and Parker would have a field day pointing out that their lakes and climate are just as nice as central Arizona's.

Arizona would seem to be in an ideal position for the future. It has plenty of land. It is twice as large as the state of Pennsylvania, but its entire population is much smaller than the Philadelphia area's. Even though only 17% of Arizona's land is in private ownership, this is equivalent to the total area of the states of New Jersey, Massachusetts, Rhode Island, and Delaware, whose combined population is five times larger. Another 13% of Arizona's land is in state ownership and can be leased for agricultural and other uses. The remaining land is controlled by the federal government and gives the state what may be its biggest asset—open space.

As we have seen, Arizona has enough renewable water to support its projected population. Just as importantly, the state's vast underground reservoirs provide unparalleled insurance against the droughts that plague other areas. With proper planning, Phoenix and Tucson could ring themselves with open space and with farms which could reuse the cities' wastewater. The nutrient value of the wastewater would provide free fertilizer for farmers and would save the energy required to manufacture fertilizer. The sale of the wastewater would save taxpayers some of the dollars required to build new treatment plants.

Much of this probably would have happened anyway if the government had not interfered and the free market system had been allowed to operate.

The free market approach has even greater implications for the water crisis of the entire Southwest, as we shall see in the next chapter.

15. Sell Water and Save Energy

Let us look at a market place approach to the impending water crisis in the Southwest. We have already seen that Arizona could use its Colorado River water on the irrigable lands near the river. This would save the taxpayers billions of dollars and thousands of kilowatts since the CAP would not be built. The market place solution would go further. To determine whether there is a more beneficial use for this water than irrigating farms, Arizona would offer its water for sale.

Our previous analysis hopefully has left little doubt that municipal and industrial uses of water provide a much higher economic return than agricultural uses. Thus Arizona could get a much higher return by selling the water instead of either building the CAP or even using the water to irrigate lands near the Colorado River. The next question is who is the most likely buyer? Presumably it is California, since most of Arizona's CAP water supply will come from water southern California has been using. This water is being delivered through the Colorado River Aqueduct, which is already in place. It is being distributed to Los Angeles and 126 other cities in southern California by the Metropolitan Water District (MWD).

If the CAP goes into operation, the MWD would lose nearly 60% of its allotment of Colorado River water. This sounds ominous and the MWD has been using this loss to the CAP to promote construction of the Delta-Peripheral

Canal to bring more water from northern to southern
California. California has contracts to deliver 4 maf to the
southern part of the state through the State Water Project
by 1994, but without the Delta Canal it has the ability to
deliver only 2 maf. In 1982 California voters rejected the
Delta project, at least for the present. The cost estimates
for this project range from 5 billion to more than 11 billion
dollars.

In addition to this economic cost, California water projects have created considerable environmental controversy.
One issue revolves around the Delta Canal as a threat to
the few remaining free flowing rivers in northern California,
such as the Eel River. That canal would provide the means
to transport more water to water-hungry southern California. Another debate centers around the drying up of Mono
Lake and the Owens Valley to provide water for Los
Angeles. It certainly appears that California has the incentive to purchase Arizona's water. In fact, a reduced CAP
was considered as one of the alternatives to the Delta Canal.
It was rejected rather abruptly for "political reasons." Obviously there was no incentive foreseen that would make
Arizona want to forego the CAP. But there are few stronger
incentives than money.

So we have the CAP costing Arizona $1.4 billion and the
U.S. taxpayer $1.7 billion (in 1977 dollars) and California
spending more billions of tax dollars to make up for their
loss of water to Arizona. A market place approach could
instead provide a profit for Arizona and a savings to the
U.S., and especially California and Arizona taxpayers.

The cost of providing "new water" to southern California
has been estimated at more than $600/af. The Colorado
River Aqueduct can transport 1.2 maf, but deliveries will
be reduced to .55 maf when CAP goes on line. If Arizona
would decide to forego the CAP and sell or lease her .65
maf to California, the state could realize an annual income
of well over $100 million, after adjusting for the cost of
delivery through the existing aqueduct.

Arizona would still have entitlement to enough water to
permit it to increase its agricultural production by irrigating
lands along the Colorado River. This would permit the

dispersal of its future growth. Possibly the greatest incentive to both states would be the saving of that other precious resource, energy.

If both states complete their planned projects, billions of gallons of water will be pumped uphill each year to a height seven times higher than the Washington Monument. The total CAP pump lift is 2,100 feet, while California would have to lift its replacement water approximately 3,500 feet. The proposed alternative would use only the existing California aqueduct with a pump lift of 1,600 feet. The resulting savings in energy would be enough to support a city of approximately a million residents.

Fig. 37 Interrelated Arizona-California water projects. *Brian Evans.*

This proposal is not really that earth-shaking. Arizona has already contracted to sell energy to California. The largest nuclear power plant in the nation is being built 50 miles west of Phoenix. The three units of the Palo Verde Nuclear generating plant will each produce 1,270 megawatts, more than half of which will be sold to other states. California has agreed to buy almost one-third of the total capacity. The water to cool the Palo Verde plant, of course, comes from Arizona's supplies.

Looking at the broader picture, California is essentially buying Arizona energy in order to pump water uphill from northern to southern California to make up for the water lost to the CAP. Furthermore, the water needs projected by the Arizona Water Commission to cool power plants in the Phoenix area by 2020 A.D. are the equivalent to one-quarter of the CAP's projected supply. Thus CAP water will be pumped uphill to produce energy that will be sent back downhill to provide the energy needed by California to pump water uphill to make up for the water taken by CAP in the first place. Selling CAP water to California certainly seems simpler and will save energy as well as tax dollars.

It is a widespread belief that insurmountable legal impediments prevent states from selling their water. Law professor Ralph W. Johnson addressed the legalities of interbasin transfers in a 1971 analysis for the National Water Commission. One of the principal consultants to the commission and "widely recognized as an authority on the legal aspects of weather modification and interbasin water transfers. . . ," Professor Johnson concluded:

We believe that the states in the area of origin have a salable interest in the water flowing within their borders, at least if the federal government cooperates in the market exchange arrangement.

One would think that Washington would cooperate since the government could save billions of tax dollars by not completing the CAP and the Delta Canal.

Most rivers that might serve as a source for an inter-regional transfer . . . flow through or along several states. How do we know, on a given river, how much water state "A" can offer in a market exchange? The answers . . . can be determined in any one of three different ways: (1) By an apportionment compact among the states sharing the river of origin, (2) by interstate litigation among those states, or (3) by congressional apportionment among those states.

Note that while any one of these is adequate, Arizona and California have met all three conditions. The 1922 Colorado River Compact was the first interstate stream compact in the nation's history. The 1963 Supreme Court case of Arizona vs. California was the interstate litigation. Congressional apportionment occurred, also for the first time, with the passage of the Boulder Canyon Project Act of 1928. The rest of the states in the Colorado River Basin have met at least the first requirement.

The interrelationship between water and energy manifests itself in many ways. Again Arizona provides a prime example. The large dams on the Colorado River provide some of the cheapest energy in the state. An Arizona law gives irrigation districts first priority to it. As a result, urban residents get little of this inexpensive electricity and so must pay many times more for their energy. The irrigation districts use this cheap energy to mine groundwater. They then claim they need CAP water because they must pump water from deeper and deeper wells. Meanwhile the large dams on the Colorado River which produce the cheap energy evaporate as much water as the CAP is supposed to deliver, creating a demand for the importation of more water.

Naturally, it is the taxpayer who pays for this foolishness. Here again the market place solution could relieve the burden. If the energy from the Colorado River dams was offered for sale to the highest bidder, its price would rise to the market level. This would force the irrigation districts to either conserve water, grow more valuable crops, or go out of business. The resulting reduction in groundwater mining would show that the CAP is not needed.

This solution could even result in a reduction in the national debt. Comparatively, the Colorado River energy is so cheap because the dams were built years ago and are almost paid off. The dams were funded by the U.S. taxpayers, and it seems only fair that the increased revenues should be used for the benefit of the entire nation. Using the profits from the free-market sale of energy to reduce the national debt could reduce interest rates and reduce inflation. Such a proposal was introduced in Congress but was rejected by a narrow margin in 1984.

Water can also affect where energy is produced and the process used to produce it. A 1974 U.S. Geological Survey report on "Water Demands for Expanding Energy Development" notes that ". . . in arid parts of the Colorado River Basin, limited water supplies will dictate economies in water use and affect plant siting." Fossil-fueled electric plants use less water than nuclear plants. In its 1979 Final Report of the Committee on Nuclear and Alternative Energy Systems, the National Academy of Sciences confirmed this:

Per unit output, today's conventional nuclear reactors require 50% more water than those burning fossil fuel. . . . On the other hand, steps can be taken to find locations where water is in fact still available, and to place increased demand at these locations, insofar as that is feasible.

As we've already seen, there are abundant supplies of fossil fuel in the Upper Basin, and the demand for more water to produce it could increase in the near future. This could provide an even better market than California, and Arizona would be wise to lease its CAP water to California for a specified number of years only. This free market approach to water could thus not only save substantial amounts of energy, it could also help the nation produce more energy.

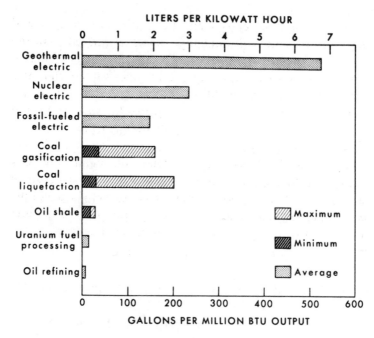

Fig. 38 Water consumption in refining and conversion processess. *U.S. Geological Survey.*

Selling its portion of CAP water to California could provide more than enough revenue to eliminate Arizona's state property tax. It could also provide the revenue to retire the farmlands that are mining the groundwater in Arizona. In 1979 the Arizona Water Commission proposed purchase and retirement of existing farms as a method of reducing groundwater mining, and this concept was subsequently incorporated into the state's new groundwater code. It was then estimated that land could be acquired for $1,000 per acre.

The goal of the code is to eliminate groundwater mining in the Phoenix and Tucson area. Even with 20% conservation and the CAP, the commission's 1977 report indicates that 200,000 acres will have to be retired by 2020 A.D. The code only permits levying a fee of "not greater than" $2/af beginning in 2006 A.D. to accomplish this. One can only speculate on the value of the land at that date, but it would take well over a century to solve the problem. The other (and more likely) solution would entail making the general taxpayer pay.

Selling CAP water to California for only 5 years could provide Arizona with enough revenue to purchase all the irrigated land in central Arizona that is dependent upon mining groundwater. It should be pointed out that this revenue is less than one-fifth of the capital cost of the CAP, which will only provide enough water, at best, to permit elimination of two-thirds of the groundwater mining.

There are, of course, many other uses for this revenue. One that we have not yet considered, but ought now look at, is that the money could help solve the problems of some of our most "truly needy" Americans. As we will see in the next chapter, this could be a most practical and, according to some, the most ethical use of these revenues.

16. Welfare or Water?

Most American Indian tribes did not subscribe to the white man's concept of private property and the concept of buying and selling land and water. In 1854 when President Pierce asked the Spokane Indians to sell their land in exchange for the creation of a reservation, their spokesman, Seattle, asked:

How can you buy the sky, the warmth of the land? The idea is strange to us. If we do not own the freshness of the air and the sparkle of the water, how can you buy them? This shining water that moves in the streams and rivers is not just water but the blood of our children.

In a 1978 article presented before an American Society of Civil Engineers conference, California attorney Sanford Smith summarized our legal treatment of the native American water rights:

The decision-making process regarding Indian water rights has been notable for one factor . . . the almost total lack of participation by Indian people in the process. Non-Indian judges have decided Indian rights, non-Indian legislators have made the laws, non-Indian attorneys have argued both sides of the cases. The crowning insult is that the result of this process is known as Indian water law.

Arizona has more Indians living on reservations than any other state in the nation. Most Americans are familiar with only the Apaches and the Navajos, but there are a total of 16 tribes in Arizona. These native Americans were finally confined to 19 reservations. Their median family income in

1980 was estimated at less than \$8,000, which is only 40% of the statewide median. About 60% of Arizona's Indians are classified as poor.

The Indians were not always so impoverished. Few Americans have heard of the Pima and Maricopa tribes, probably because these tribes cooperated with, rather than fought, the early white settlers. They lived along the Gila River, which merges with the Salt River a few miles downstream from Phoenix. A century ago the Gila was a perenially flowing river traversing the entire east-west length of Arizona. It was the favored route by white prospectors and pioneers on their journey to California.

Travelers were fed and rested by the Pimas, who were the leading farmers of the Southwest. They were described as a peaceful, generous and friendly people. The following account from an award-winning Phoenix television documentary presents a vivid description of the fate of their culture.

In the early 1700s, a Jesuit missionary following in the footsteps of Father Kino visited the lands of the Pima and Maricopa Indians. He reported an abundance of corn, beans, pumpkins, watermelons, wheat, and cotton. 150 years later, a captain in the Mormon batallion reported cultivated lands could be seen 15 or 20 miles in every direction. During the next two decades, the Indians increased their cultivation to provide food for the Butterfield Overland Mail Company and the early settlers. Harvests measured in the millions of pounds and cattle numbered over 2,000 head. At one point, millions of pounds of surplus wheat were sold to the U.S. on credit.

The loyalty of these Indians was so trusted that they were given arms to protect the settlers when the Army moved out during the Civil War. General McDowell described these people as having done more to give peace and security to Arizona than all the white troops combined. After the Civil War, they provided troops to protect settlers in the upper reach of the Gila River from hostile Apaches.

Ironically, these same settlers were diverting water from the upper Gila, depleting the river downstream through the Indian lands. Numerous dispatches by the Indian agents told of these illegal diversions between 1870 and 1895 but Washington returned only promises. Finally the Indians had barely enough water for themselves and their animals to drink and were impoverished and facing starvation. One of the tribal members summed up the situation with the following speech:

"For hundreds of years my people have lived on the banks of the Gila River. We have always been honest and peaceful and have supported ourselves and never asked for any help from the Great White Father at Washington. Until the past few years we have always had plenty of water to irrigate our farms and never knew what want was. We always had grain stored up for a full year's supply. We were happy and contented. Since the white man came and built the big canals and ditches, we have no water for crops. The government refuses to give us food and we do not ask for it. We only ask for water for we prefer to earn our own living if we can. . . ."

By 1895 the situation was so desperate that the government distributed 225,000 pounds of wheat among the Pimas as rations. This practice continued, and eventually wells were constructed. In 1924 Congress authorized construction of the San Carlos Reservoir upstream on the Gila River. This was supposed to provide enough water to irrigate 100,000 acres but has only supplied enough to farm 20,000 acres. Today slightly more than one-quarter of the Gila River Reservation's arable acres are irrigated.

Arizona's surface water law holds that the first to put surface water to beneficial use has the right to its continued use. It should be obvious from the previous discussion that the Pima Indians should have the best water rights in the state. They were never conquered (at least by warfare) and have maintained their sovereignty through the centuries.

The typical fate of western Indians is their conquest and movement to reservations. Since they were generally nomadic, and this was hardly compatible with staying on reservations, they were taught farming. In 1908 in the Winters decision, the U.S. Supreme Court held that it was implied at the time of the establishment of a reservation that enough water was reserved for the reservation's purposes.

The Pima and other central Arizona tribes began pursuing their water rights through the courts. As it became increasingly obvious to Arizona's water interests that the Indians had substantial water rights, the amount of CAP water allocated to them increased. In 1968 it was less than 100,000 acre feet, but by 1980 this had increased to more than 300,000 acre feet.

From the standpoint of the Arizona taxpayer, it would be beneficial to give all of the CAP water to the Indians. Cities and industries have to repay the billion-dollar-plus loan with interest. Farmers repay their part of the capital cost but pay no interest. Indians do not have to repay even the capital cost. So Arizona would get CAP water at no cost to the local taxpayers.

This could also give the CAP a purpose. The federal government has a trust obligation to the Indians, and this would provide Washington the opportunity to fulfill that responsibility. The resulting water supply could permit the tribes to maintain their culture, at least for the duration of the CAP supply. According to the 1978 U.S. General Accounting Office report to Congress on "Reserved Water Rights for Federal and Indian Reservations," "adequate water supplies are an important resource for improving the economic and social standing of the Indians."

The uncertainty of the CAP supply, though, should suggest caution to those tribes who are considering that project as a solution to their water claims. Fortunately there are other ways to right the wrongs that placed the Pima and Maricopa tribes on welfare. Since the early Arizona settlers essentially stole the water from these Indians, perhaps Arizona should make reparations. The state could use the proceeds from the sale of its CAP water to retire the upstream farmlands that depleted the flow of the Gila River a century ago. The river's environment would be restored, and the Indians could get off welfare and maintain their culture indefinitely. History could repeat itself as they once again provide food to the settlers—in the rapidly growing Phoenix area.

The federal government provided another alternative when it fulfilled its trust responsibility to the Ak Chin Maricopa tribe. These Indians reside on a small reservation at the southwest corner of the Pima Indian Gila River reservation. Virtually the entire 21,000 acre reservation is arable, but only around 20% was irrigated in the 1970s. Non-Indian irrigation districts surround the reservation, and the combined Indian and non-Indian pumping has resulted in some of the deepest wells in central Arizona. In 1981 the government agreed to pump 85,000 acre feet a year to the reservation from under land owned by the U.S. in central Arizona and deliver it to the reservation.

This solution suggests another way to get water to the Indians without CAP. There are more than a billion acre feet of groundwater in storage under the state of Arizona to a depth of 1200 feet. This is roughly 1,000 times the annual water supply that the CAP is supposed to deliver. The amount in storage under central Arizona to these depths is 500 times the CAP supply. The Bureau of Reclamation has apparently never considered groundwater as an alternative to the CAP.

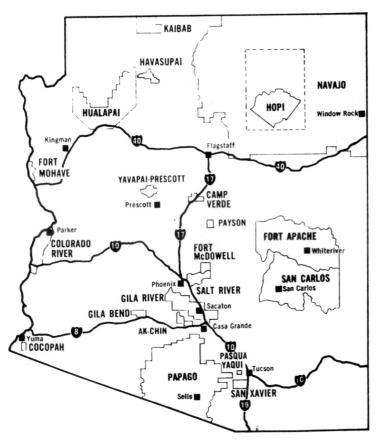

Fig. 39 Indian Reservations in Arizona. *Arizona Commission on Indian Affairs.*

Yet another option was introduced into the U.S. Senate in 1976. This bill would have used federal funds to purchase 170,000 acres of Arizona farmland with surface water rights. This would release 700,000 acre feet which would then be transferred to the tribes in satisfaction of their claims. At the previously mentioned $1,000 an acre price, this would have cost $170 million, again a fraction of the then $2.2 billion CAP cost. The bill failed to get out of the Senate.

It should be noted that the Senate proposal would have given the tribes 4.1 acre feet for each irrigated acre. The average irrigated acre in the Phoenix area consumed only 3.6 af per acre and the 1977 Arizona Water Commission study projected the water use in Pinal County, where the Gila River Reservation is located, would be 3.2 af/acre by 2020 A.D. This would require conservation, however.

Indian tribes are understandably leery of the federal government, and water projects are one of the major causes of their distrust. A prime example of this is the Pick-Sloan Plan developed jointly by the Bureau of Reclamation and the Corps of Engineers between 1940 and 1960. Three of the plan's dams flooded over 200,000 acres of profitable Sioux Creek, and Yankton reservations. In the foreword to Michael Lawson's 1982 book, *Dammed Indians*, Sioux historian Vine Deloria, Jr., writes:

The Pick-Sloan Plan was, without doubt, the single most destructive act ever perpetrated on any tribe by the United States. If it had simply been one act and had been committed only against the Sioux with the violation of only one treaty, it would be viewed as gross and unfair; but the projects eventually involved almost all tribes living on the Missouri and its major tributaries in the states of South Dakota, North Dakota, Montana, and Wyoming, and the end is still not in sight.

The bureau's plan for one dam in Arizona has the potential for an equally devastating effect on one of Arizona's Indian tribes, as we shall soon see.

17. Salinity

Three-quarters of the earth is covered with water, but only 3% of that water on the earth is fresh, and even that is a relative term. In the arid West, salinity is a major problem. Rain and snow falling on the Rocky Mountains provide virtually pure water. As it flows over land, the water dissolves minerals which are collectively called salts. Irrigation and storage in reservoirs result in evaporation of virtually pure water, concentrating the salts in the remaining water.

As the Colorado River leaves the Upper Basin just below Lake Powell, the salt concentration has already reached 600 parts per million (ppm). Seven hundred and fifty parts of salt have been concentrated in each million parts of water as the river flows out of Lake Mead. This is the water that the CAP plans to deliver to central Arizona.

The salinity of the surface water in the Phoenix area and the groundwater in the Tucson area are generally below 500 ppm. This is the recommended limit for drinking water when no other supplies are available, according to the U.S. Public Health Service. It is the highest "desirable" concentration according to the World Health Organization and the National Bureau of Health. By permitting CAP water to blend with their existing supplies, Phoenix and Tucson are polluting their own drinking water!

One of these salts, sulfate, could be particularly troublesome. The recommended limit is 250 ppm. The U.S. Geological Survey in a report on the Colorado River notes that concentrations of 200 to 300 ppm "will have a laxative effect on some of those who drink the water." CAP water supplies would contain 350 ppm. While the biological systems of those receiving a continuous supply will probably adjust, visitors might well experience diarrhea.

Government officials argue that CAP water is of better quality than the groundwater in central Arizona. Arizona Water Commission reports state that the "average" salinity of these underground supplies is 900 ppm. This average results from a range of as low as 200 ppm in the northern part of the Phoenix area to more than 3,000 ppm in the southern part. The latter is used mostly for agriculture. People should not have to drink CAP water when adequate supplies of better quality water are available. Southern California uses desalting plants to reduce the salinity of the Colorado River water they import, but central Arizona has no plans to do the same. Of course, California considers salinity its number one water quality problem while Arizona does not seem too concerned about the pollution of its water.

In 1974 Tucson estimated that the salt concentrations in CAP water would cost each household $30 to $45 a year in damages. These salts adversely affect the longevity of water heaters. It also corrodes pipes and plumbing and, in general, requires increased use of detergents, causes crusty stains in bathtubs and sinks, not to mention spots on glassware. Among other detrimental effects must be included poorer-tasting water, while effects on health are highly controversial.

Salts also have an effect on plants by encrusting the roots, thereby retarding growth and reducing crop production. In 1971 the EPA projected that this would result in losses of $4.6 million to farmers along the lower Colorado River. In 1976 the bureau estimated the present worth (at $6\frac{7}{8}\%$) of salinity damage on the Colorado River at more than a billion dollars.

The bureau of course did not undertake this study to show the detrimental effect of water salinity but rather to justify new projects to lower the salt content of the Colorado River. The Upper Basin is responsible for almost three-fourths of the salinity of the Lower Basin. More than half of this is from natural sources while the remainder is primarily attributed to irrigated agriculture. The bureau's plan to clean up the river includes the evaporation of thousands of acre feet of salty water, an endeavor to convince Upper Basin farmers to adopt more efficient irrigation practices, and of course the expenditure of more millions of tax dollars.

The largest, and most wasteful, of the bureau's desalting plans is in the Lower Basin, however. The Yuma Desalting Plant will cost the taxpayers more than $300 million dollars and consume more than 40 megawatts of energy. This plant resulted from an international incident over salinity. Mexico complained that the high salt concentration in the Colorado River as it entered her border was destroying her crops.

The major contributor to this condition was the Welton-Mohawk Irrigation District, which extends up the Gila River east of Yuma for 50 miles. The bureau created the district by diverting water from the Colorado River through a series of canals. Irrigation further concentrated the already salty river water, and by the time it flowed back into the river it had reached concentrations of 6,000 ppm.

The bureau's initial solution was to retire thousands of acres of land in the district. When compared to the cost of the desalting plant, this concept made sense. The entire 70,000 acre district could have been bought out for a fraction of the cost of the plant. This is one of the most productive areas in the United States, however, with a gross return per acre higher than Arizona as a whole, so another solution would seem to be preferable.

University of Arizona agricultural economist William Martin investigated alternatives to the problem in 1974. He found farmers were charged $12 for the first nine acre feet, whether the water was used or not. Up to 12 acre feet was being used on an acre. Obviously, one solution was to price water on an acre foot basis, although the cheap water and the loss of unused water rights would still discourage conservation.

This high water use permitted the bureau to negate the use of Arizona's remaining entitlement to the Colorado River on the thousands of acres of irrigable land near the river. Yet Professor Martin pointed out that drip irrigation and sprinkler systems could reduce this use to 4 and 5 acre feet per acre respectively. This would have resulted in an actual savings to the district of almost $10 an acre, and the resultant reduction in the return flow to the Colorado River would substantially reduce the salinity of the water delivered to Mexico.

As with the CAP, construction began on the Yuma Desalting Plant even though there were superior alternatives. Those aware of the situation can surely sympathize with the conclusion of Professor Martin:

> . . . Thus it is somewhat frustrating to watch the results of poor past planning and present political necessity bring about enormous public expenditures on structural remedies at this time. One may hope for future times when efforts will be directed toward problem causes rather than problem effects.

The future of central Arizona could be quite rosy without the CAP. With proper planning, the water supplies of the cities can be improved rather than polluted. While the salinity of the aptly named Salt River often exceeds 600 ppm, Verde River waters are only half that. At present, due to past planning centering on irrigation, the two rivers are allowed to mingle before the waters are diverted. This results in the water being delivered to the cities just meeting the 500 ppm recommended limit for drinking water.

There is enough water in the Verde to supply projected populations for the Phoenix area into the next century if it is used only for cities. It was in 1921 that Verde water was first brought to Phoenix, an event considered important enough to rate the entire front page of the local newspaper. With the damages associated with salinity, it would certainly appear economically feasible to bring more Verde River water to the Phoenix area so that every resident can enjoy the "sweet waters of the Verde" once again.

While agriculture interests might not like being limited to the salty waters of the Salt, their major interest is in the cost rather than the quality of water since major damages to most crops do not occur until salinity approaches 1,000 ppm. Pricing water based upon quality should satisfy both interests. Salt River water could be even cheaper than it is now. Excellent quality Verde water would be sold at a premium price, and these revenues could then be used to deliver more of that water to the Phoenix area.

This could provide additional benefits for both interests. Wastewater presently contains about 900 ppm of salts. With cities getting better quality water up front, the resultant wastewater would be of virtually the same salinity as present water supplies and of better quality than Salt River supplies. This would benefit agriculture, and selling these nutrient-laden waters could save the cities the cost of building new sewage treatment plants.

The salinity of existing water supplies in the Phoenix area could be decreased by reducing the amount of water evaporated in the six large reservoirs in the Salt and Verde Rivers. Most of the reservoirs are located in deep canyons, and as water levels rise small increases in storage result in large increases in surface areas. The increased evaporation results in increased salinity. Here again the policies of the Salt River Project discourage the maintenance of these reservoirs at optimum levels.

SRP annually assesses each acre of its member lands a fee. Under normal conditions, 2 af of "assessed" water are provided to each acre. Empty reservoirs would result in no assessed water, while full lakes would provide more water — for the same annual assessment fee. It is obviously to the benefit of the large landowners, who, remember, elect the Board of the SRP, to maximize storage and thus minimize their water costs. To illustrate, the 1980 assessment was $13 per acre, so if two acre feet (af) were available, the price of water would be $6.50 af. If only one af was provided, the price would be $13 af. This would result in a difference of more than one thousand dollars a year for a 160 acre farm.

This complex management system obviously militates against the operation of the reservoirs to reduce evaporation and provide higher quality water. From what we've seen, Arizona seems more concerned with quantity than quality when it comes to water. Virtually no concern has been expressed about the CAP's pollution of central Arizona's water supply. The CAP's four dams would evaporate still more water and further concentrate the salts. The largest reservoir, Orme, would evaporate 29,000 acre feet of water and increase salinity by 65 ppm.

This is only one of the adverse effects of Orme Dam, which has been called the worst part of the CAP. It has been said that there is something in the CAP to offend almost everyone, and Orme is decidedly the worst part of the CAP.

VI THE WAR OVER ORME DAM

18. The First Battle: The CCAP and the Tubers

The case of the Orme Dam controversy in the Phoenix area provides a perfect example of the difficulties of opposing a massive bureaucracy like the Bureau of Reclamation. Someone once said that a bureaucracy's primary purpose is to perpetuate its own existence; all other considerations are secondary. The Bureau of Reclamation must build to survive. The Orme Dam case demonstrates the Hydra-like nature of the bureau; cut off one head (dam) and two more appear in its place. The bureau appears to have lost all awareness of its responsibility to the nation and its taxpayers, who, after all, pay the bills. It acts as if it were a sovereign entity, answerable to no one.

Take the following narrative and analysis, if you will, as a cautionary tale with both good and bad sides. On the one hand, the lengths to which the bureau and its supporters (chiefly developers and farmers and the politicians that are their public voice) will go to hoodwink the public is clear. When one argument fails, they adopt another and another and another, often to the point of absurdity. They do not give up. On the other hand, the benefits of public education and tireless vigilance is also clear: the Orme Dam and its alternatives were stopped repeatedly. But the bureau has always returned to the attack.

It must be remembered that Orme Dam is *still authorized*; funding has been withdrawn but can be reinstated whenever Congress decides that the political atmosphere is safe.

In 1968 Congress authorized "Orme Dam or a suitable alternative" as part of the Central Arizona Project. The stated purpose of the dam was to regulate CAP flows, protect the Phoenix area from floods, and provide increased water-based recreation. Few Arizonans knew about the dam, but within a decade it would become the most controversial issue of the day.

The dam's primary function was to store CAP water pumped uphill during the winter for use during the peak demand periods in the summer. This "regulatory storage" would result in a 10% increase in the amount of water delivered by the CAP. When the energy crisis arrived in the 1970s, it was also argued that pumping during the winter would save valuable energy in the summer.

The earliest opposition to the dam came from the local chapter of the Audubon Society and a newly-formed citizens' taxpayer group. Incorporated in 1973, Citizens Concerned About the Project (CCAP) officially opposed the CAP in 1974 and called Orme Dam "the worst part of the CAP." These groups argued that the Bureau of Reclamation should make a separate economic analysis of the dam rather than lumping it in with the overall CAP justification.

After the bureau was finally forced into a separate analysis, officials reluctantly admitted that they could not use their $200 an acre foot (af) figure for municipal and industrial water. That "demand" would already have been satisfied with CAP water. They agreed that almost all Orme water would be for agricultural use. However, the bureau insisted upon the figure of $100 af since that was the inflated value they used for CAP agricultural water.

It was pointed out that four independent studies showed that the value of additional water brought to the Phoenix area was only $15/af, that this should be the value of CAP water for agriculture, and that Orme would bring in additional water which would logically be worth even less. To make a long story short, the bureau came down to $34/af at one point but then raised it to $67/af. They finally dropped

"Our exorbitant figure should justify building it, Congressman."

Fig. 40 *Dave Campbell.*

the argument altogether and used energy savings to justify this regulatory storage. Opponents countered this by suggesting the elimination of the entire CAP since its water supply could not be economically justified either, and substantially greater amounts of energy would be saved.

The bureau also argued that Orme was needed to protect the Phoenix area from floods. Orme opponents countered this by pointing out that in 1958 the U.S. Army Corps of Engineers recommended levees and channel improvements as the solutions to the "flood menace" that exists along the Salt River.

During this dialogue the bureau awarded a contract for construction of part of the CAP canal, the construction of which, opponents had claimed, would eliminate one of the alternatives to Orme Dam. The Maricopa Audubon Society and CCAP joined forces and, with several individual plaintiffs, filed a lawsuit asking that the bureau be enjoined from building that portion of the CAP aqueduct until an environmental impact statement was completed on the dam. The suit was filed in June 1975 and never was decided by the

court. The bureau awarded the contract and permitted construction to continue until it was completed. At that point
the lawsuit was "moot."

As a non-profit organization, CCAP depended on its vol-
unteers to educate the public by distributing literature at
shopping centers and, during this period, at the Salt River.
Thousands of people from the Phoenix area congregated at
that river on summer weekends to escape the 115-degree
heat of the city. Most of these river people were from the
younger generation, and their favorite recreation was float-
ing the river on inner tubes. The 10-mile stretch of Salt
River downstream from the four dams to the river's junction
with the Verde River was the favored area. As many as
10,000 "tubers" enjoyed this stretch of water on a typical
summer Sunday.

The tubers were not happy to hear that Orme would
make their flowing river a placid lake. They argued that
there were already six lakes on the river system for sailboat
and water skiing enthusiasts. Orme proponents cited government studies showing that Arizona needed more flat
water recreation, but opponents demonstrated that the
shortage in the Phoenix area was not of flat water but of
facilities—parking areas, boat launching ramps, etc. It was
simply a question of access.

Proponents then stressed the number of drownings on
the river, implying that such a dangerous recreation area
deserved to be destroyed. The tubers again did their home-
work and countered by pointing out that more people die
in their bathtubs than in Arizona's rivers. They also noted
that the river would be replaced by a lake, and people drown
in lakes as well. Finally they argued that it was absurd for
the bureau to exaggerate the benefits of lake recreation while
ignoring the benefits of river recreation that would be lost
through the creation of the lake.

The bureau chose to hold the public hearing on the draft
environmental impact statement for Orme Dam and Reservoir in July 1976. Some Audubon members considered this
ironic since the dam would flood the natural habitat of our
national symbol, the bald eagle, and the federal government
would make its case during the bicentennial celebration!

Many Phoenicians had left the valley to escape the 115-degree heat, but the tubers helped swell the ranks of the hundreds of citizens who attended the hearing.

The atmosphere of the hearing was definitely anti-Orme. The speakers pointed out that one of the "alternatives" mentioned in the statement was the very project that the lawsuit had centered upon and they noted that many of the 15 alternatives presented were merely variations of Orme, either at different sites or different heights. But the major event of the hearing resulted from CCAP's interception of a report that very morning. An Arizona Bureau of Mines study stated that the Orme Dam site was highly faulted. (This was shortly after the Teton Dam failure.) When the hearing resumed after lunch the bureau found their Orme Dam model interlaced with the reported fault zones. Of even greater visual impact was the report on the front page of the state's largest newspaper that Orme could be an unsafe dam.

The battle had been won by Orme opponents but the war was just beginning. The greater upheavals to come were signaled by the testimony of John Williams. He told the government that they would have to shoot him with a "silver bullet" to get him to move from the land which Orme would inundate. His real name was Kehedawah, and he was an elder of the Fort McDowell Yavapai Indian community. Their reservation would be flooded by Orme reservoir.

19. The Second Battle: The Indians

Only a century ago the ancestors of the 400 residents of the Fort McDowell Indian Reservation were a nation of several thousand. All of central and western Arizona was the home of the Yavapai Indians, but today the Fort McDowell reservation measures only 10 miles by 4 miles.

When the Yavapai first encountered the white man, they called themselves the "people" or human beings. Unfortunately, their word for this, "A'baja", sounds like "Apache." Anthropoligist Dr. Sigrid Khera, editor of the book *The Yavapai of Fort McDowell*, explains the result of this misunderstanding:

Calling the Yavapai "Apache" was a very convenient excuse for the English speaking Americans to kill the Yavapai and take over their land. The Apache fought with guns when the white people

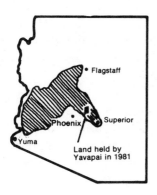

Fig. 41 Approximate area of land held by Yavapai Indians in Arizona in 1873. *Dr. Sigrud Khera.*

wanted to push them out of their land. So the white people considered them their worst enemies. . . . The Yavapai had no guns.
They had only bow and arrow and club. They knew they could
not fight army guns with bow and arrow and club. So the chiefs
promised the white people not to fight them. . . . But the Yavapai
land contained lots of gold and copper and other valuable metals.
The land was good for cattle ranching. Along the rivers and
springs there was good land for farming. The white people wanted
that land for themselves alone and the Indians out. By calling
the Yavapai "Apache" they felt it was only all right to kill them
and push them off their land.

The Indians moved to reservations but left after many
died from smallpox as a result of being given infected clothes.
The soldiers then lured the Yavapai to the east of Prescott
with promises of wagons and horses. Upon their arrival the
soldiers started shooting, and today the area is known as
Skull Valley after the skulls of the murdered Yavapai.

This was the tribe that was involved in the "Battle of
Skeleton Cave." No soldiers were even hurt during this
"battle" but a band of Yavapai, including women and children, were wiped out as soldiers fired into the cave. The
Indians were killed as bullets ricocheted off the walls. The
skeletons of the Indians gave the cave its name. Bloody
Basin is another Arizona place that owes its name to a
"battle." Here the soldiers slaughtered Yavapai who were
peacefully gathering mescal.

In March of 1875 the Yavapai were herded together and
forced to march more than a hundred miles to the San
Carlos Apache Reservation in eastern Arizona. They were
moved there because the white settlers wanted their land
and water and told Washington these "Apaches" should be
sent to an Apache reservation. Even the old and sick, preg-
nant women, and those with babies had to march on foot.
They were forced to ford icy, swollen rivers and were shot
and poisoned on the way. Few made it.

In San Carlos the men were told that if they served as
scouts they eventually would be allowed to go back home
to their own land. So they all joined the army. Some time
after their arrival the government ordered all Yavapai children sent to boarding schools. Some returned only many
years later while others never came back.

Twenty-five years later the Yavapai returned to Fort McDowell only to find Mexicans and Anglos farming the remaining portion of their once large land. The Indians had to live on the barren hillsides while they worked for these farmers, even though the old military reservation had been set aside as a reservation for the Mohave and Yavapai Apaches.

In 1903 the tribe cut wood and sold baskets to make enough money to send their chief Kapalwa, whom they called Yuma Frank, and three tribal members to Washington. They had to sneak away early in the morning since the superintendent of the Indian Office had ordered them not to go under threat of imprisonment. They returned with a document setting aside the abandoned Camp McDowell military reservation for the Indians. It was signed by President Theodore Roosevelt on September 15, 1903.

That same year, the Salt River Valley Water Users Association, now generally known as SRP, was founded, and in 1905 petitioned Judge Kent to apportion the waters of the Salt and Verde Rivers. In 1910 the Kent Decree was handed down. It recognized the rights of Fort McDowell, but the federal judge added that the government intended to move the Indians and the rights would then be transferred to others.

From 1910 to 1930, the government tried to move the Yavapai to the Pima Indian Reservation on the Salt River. In 1911 a flood destroyed the Yavapai's irrigation system and the government refused to make repairs. Officials said the Indians should move, refused them any aid, and even closed their dayschool in Fort McDowell.

Fortunately, in a sense, a Yavapai child known as Wassaja had been captured and sold to a white man in the 1870s. He was educated in the East and became a famous doctor in Chicago. Dr. Montezuma helped his people, who could not read English, avoid legal pitfalls and advised them not to move since they would lose their rights to the "sweet waters of the Verde."

In 1921, two years before his death, Dr. Montezuma warned his people that the efforts of the whites to take over their reservaton would continue. On March 24 he wrote:

When I was there (Ft. McDowell) last fall, engineers were sounding the Verde River east of the McDowell mountain. Do you know what that means? Some day a dam will be built and the McDowell land will be flooded and the water will be used for drinking water for the Salt River Valley people. No wonder the McDowell Indians are hoodwinked and urged to move to Salt River reservation. White people's heads are long; they can see many years ahead. . . .

This prophecy came true 47 years later when Congress authorized the construction of Orme Dam, which would flood two-thirds of the reservation.

In 1973, five years after the dam was authorized, the Bureau of Reclamation finally met with the Fort McDowell community and informed them of the plans to build the dam that would flood their land. They were offered more than $30 million, which would amount to $70,000 for each resident. Many individual Indians spoke out against the dam, emphasizing that they wanted their land, not money. In essence, they said "just leave us alone."

Tribal members contacted a concerned Phoenix-area housewife and told her of their plight. Mrs. Carolina Butler, a Mexican-American homemaker, encouraged the native Americans to notify the government directly that they were not willing to move. She also provided them with necessary information on the dam and explained the way the system functions.

In 1975 individual tribal members took a poll of the residents which showed 140 opposed, one in favor, and 8 with no opinion. The tribal council had not taken a stand on the dam and the poll apparently did not sway them. Five individuals paid their own fare to Washington to inform Congress of the poll. Among these tribal members were tribal elder, John Williams and his granddaughter, Kimberly. John was the son of Tom Suramma, who had accompanied Yuma Frank on his trip to Washington in 1903.

Early in 1976 the bureau presented five "educational" seminars to the tribe about the advantages and disadvantages of selling their land. The program began with a 20-minute movie on the CAP entitled "Project Rescue" which was prepared by the Central Arizona Project Association, the private CAP lobbying group. In September another referendum was held which included tribal members who had chosen to live off the reservation. The voting age was lowered to 18 years. By a vote of 144 to 57 the Yavapais again rejected the sale of their land for the Orme Dam site.

In 1977 President Carter withdrew all funding for Orme Dam and ordered a study of "suitable alternatives." His major reason for this action was the opposition of the Fort McDowell Indians. Governor Castro of Arizona then appointed a representative group of citizens to work with the state government on alternatives. Among the other information presented to this group was that the flood control aspect of the dam would return only 23 cents in benefits for each dollar invested. Facts are of little import during the emotions of an actual flood, however.

20. The Third Battle: The Rains Came

In March and December of 1978 and again in February of 1980, the rains came. The Salt River Project released water from its upstream dams into the normally dry Salt River bed that bisects the Phoenix area. Several lives were lost, traffic was disrupted as bridges were washed out, and millions of dollars in damages were incurred.

Fig. 42 Phoenix area dams and flooded communities. *Maricopa Audubon Society.*

During the largest flood in February 1980, evacuation of residents near the river was considered imminent. Only two of twenty major streets across the Salt River in the metropolitan area remained open, and for many weeks motorists lined up for hours to cross the river. It was estimated that $56 million in damages had been sustained.

Some residents blamed the flood on the Salt River Project, claiming that the dams should be used for flood control as well as storage. The famous attorney, Melvin Belli, agreed and sued SRP. SRP continued to maintain that it was not in the business of flood control and that its dams were not designed for that purpose. A 1983 consulting engineer's study found, however, that ". . . for the size of any floods on record, proper reservoir operation could significantly attenuate the peak flow." Early in 1984 SRP arranged an out of court settlement just before the case was scheduled for trial.

To many, including politicians and the state's largest newspaper, the floods seemed a golden opportunity to attempt to resurrect Orme dam, based on the alleged need for more flood control. Distortion of the facts began immediately. The news media and the politicans pointed to the "devastating" 1978 floods that killed more than a dozen people. While the highest incidence of drownings associated with release of water into the Salt River did occur in 1978, the deaths resulted from people going to the river rather than the river inundating them.

The highest mortality should have occurred during the March 1978 flood since the public was totally unprepared. The release of water was the largest since 1920, when Roosevelt was the only dam on the Salt and Verde Rivers. Yet only two deaths occurred there. One of the fatalities resulted from an attempted daredevil leap by a vehicle, a la Evil Kneivel. The second occurred when a four-wheel drive vehicle attempted to ford the river. Both drove around road barricades.

Four fatalities were blamed on the December 1978 flood. Three people drowned when their four-wheel drive vehicle attempted to ford the river. The barricades were reported "removed by unknown persons." The fourth death was caused by a fire in the operations facility at one of the dams.

It takes water many hours to travel from the upstream dams to the urban Phoenix area. This gives plenty of time to warn the residents, set up barricades, etc. Almost any flow in the river will result in fatalities if people choose to ignore the warnings. While Orme Dam would have reduced the flows by more than half, it would not have made people any less reckless and foolhardy. Fatalities probably would still have occurred. No deaths resulted from the February 1980 event even though it resulted in the largest release of water. Flood fatalities were clearly not linked to the amount of water in the river.

The release of water from the upstream dams did cause considerable property damage. In the largest flood in 1980, almost half the damage was related to roads and bridges, with one-third of this attributed to traffic delays.

The Tempe bridge across the Salt River, which was built in the 1930s, easily withstood the floods, leading to the idea that "they just don't build bridges like they used to." But few bothered to consider that the Central Avenue bridge was built in 1975 and also withstood the floods. The Tempe bridge could be considered the better of the two but only because it is situated at the only place in the valley where its foundation could be built on solid rock. The Central Avenue bridge withstood the same flood flows and its foundation is built upon sand and gravel.

Eleven Salt River bridges connecting north and south Phoenix were destroyed by the three large releases of 1978-80. The largest bridge was designed to pass a flow of only 35,000 cubic feet per second (cfs) while the flows ranged from 120,000 cfs to 180,000 cfs. Politicans and government officials explained that the small bridges were built because no water had flowed in the Salt River through Phoenix for almost 30 years—between 1938 and 1965. Two dams on the formerly free-flowing Verde River were completed after the 1938 flood, and the valley was feeling quite complacent. Building bridges across a dry river could almost be considered ludicrous.

In December 1965, however, the Salt River Project released 65,000 cfs from its upstream dams. For a while only the Tempe bridge remained open while the other bridges were closed for repairs. Traffic was disrupted for several weeks.

This was a relatively small flood that, based on historical flows, could be expected to recur at least every 20 years. Yet in the next ten years, ten new bridges were built that would pass flows of only 7,000 cfs to 35,000 cfs. Fortunately, the Central Avenue bridge was replaced by a span that would permit passage of very large flows which should be exceeded only once every 100 years. In other words, such a flood would have only a one percent chance of occurrence in any one year.

Politicians and government officials also slyly claimed the small bridges were built in anticipation of the construction of Orme Dam. But four of the bridges were built before Orme was even authorized by Congress, and Orme was designed to release 50,000 cfs into the river, which would have incapacitated all ten bridges. Hardly a convincing argument.

While the proponents clamored for the dam, it was pointed out that most Phoenicians would not ever have known there was a flood if there had been better bridges. The public outcry of "more bridges, not more dams" finally forced the provision of funds for a dozen large bridges which would permit passage of flows even larger than that of February 1980.

In March 1982, SRP again released water into the river. All the unbridged crossings were closed, but by then five new bridges had been added to the three existing large bridges. Traffic delays were negligible as the public continued business as usual. The cost of the five new bridges was $23 million while Orme Dam's 1980 price tag was $598 million.

Other damages resulted from the floods, of course. One-fifth of the 1980 damage was incurred by public facilities built in the floodplain. This included the airport, sewage treatment facilities, and other government and utility-owned property. But even here, it is not clearly evident that this damage could be unequivocally attributed to unforeseen flooding. Of all sectors of society, the government and large utilities were best equipped to anticipate flooding.

It can only be assumed that they decided construction was worth the risk. The February 1980 event could be expected to occur every 50 years. The politicians and the staffs of these public entities presumably must have decided that repairing or replacing these facilities every 50 years or so was more economical than protecting them or than locating them in higher-priced real estate outside the flood-prone areas.

The 1965 event was half the size of the 1980 occurrence and almost the same proportion of damage was attributed to government and the utilities. A full one-third of the 1965 damage was sustained by companies mining gravel in the river bottom. Surely they, too, should have expected to incur flood damages. It is interesting to note that failure of the freeway bridge in 1980 has been linked to these gravel mining operations. The state legislature has been unsuccessful in its attempts to regulate these companies.

Only 3% of the February 1980 damage was incurred by residential and commercial interests, while industrial damage other than gravel mining accounted for less than 2%. That this damage was not greater can be attributed to the floodplain ordinance passed by the state legislature in 1973, and some of the damages that did occur resulted from the lack of enforcement of this law by local government.

The Arizona floodplain law essentially defines the floodplain as the lowlands adjoining the channel of a watercourse

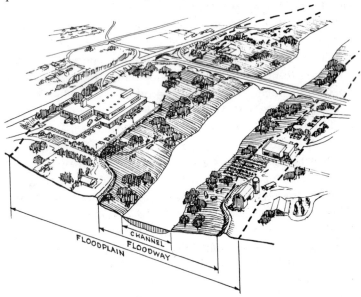

Fig. 43 Permitted uses within a 100-year floodplain. *Dave Campbell.*

which may be covered by floodwater from a 100-year flood. It generally prohibits development within the "floodway," which is the channel itself and those neighboring areas subject to frequent flooding. Activities within the floodway area are restricted to agriculture, parking, recreation, and open space. Development within the floodplain but outside the floodway is permitted as long as the minimum floor elevation is above the high water line of the 100-year flood.

The cities in the Phoenix area did an admirable job of enforcing this law, but the county was less responsible. Three years after the legislation was passed, the county supervisors permitted a Phoenix couple to locate their mobile home in the floodplain even though the "property would be under 7 feet of water in a 100-year flood."

The couple had just bought the 9-acre parcel and claimed they were not aware it was in the floodplain and did not know about the floodplain restrictions. They agreed to record a waiver absolving the county of liability and said they planned to farm the land which was 3 miles outside the Phoenix city limits.

The newspaper article reporting this waiver noted that others were trying to obtain an exemption. The parcel owned by the couple was inundated during the 1980 flood. Whether they, like so many others, were given federal relief aid is not known, but they certainly added to the tally of flood damages. One must wonder if they paid a bargain price for their land since it was in the floodplain—and whether they appreciated the county's "benevolence" after the flooding.

That people who move into the floodplain deserve to get flooded is the prevailing opinion in America and has merit where there is a flowing river and the danger is obvious. This policy of "caveat emptor" (let the buyer beware) is often applied with more consideration in today's highly complex society, however.

Prior to the completion of the Roosevelt Dam in 1910, the Salt was a free-flowing river as it passed through Phoenix. The 6-foot-long Colorado River Squawfish, now an endangered species, swam in its waters and was used as fertilizer on the farmer's fields. By 1946 the sixth dam was completed upstream on the Salt and Verde Rivers and the "river ran dry" and began blending in with the surrounding desert. Surely a prospective homebuyer would have a difficult time imagining that a great river once flowed near his property—and could flow again.

The community of Allenville provides a perfect example. It was founded in the early 1940s for migratory black farm workers who wanted something better than life in a labor camp. They were unable to live in the nearby community of Buckeye because of restricted housing patterns. Unfortunately they located within the floodplain of the river. Worse yet, part of Allenville was within the floodway itself.

The floodway of a river, as has been stated, is the part subject to frequent flooding. For the Salt, this occurs much more often than the projected 100-year debacle. As a result, 51 families were evacuated during the 1965 release and again in March 1978. Finally the December 1978 event resulted in the abandonment of the community and the relocation of the residents.

The Corps of Engineers investigated solutions to the problem. One consisted of clearing the channel of the river bed, but this would have lowered the water level of a 100-year flood by only 2 feet. A second would have required 10-foot-high levees. Another would require the raising of a sizable portion of the community above the level of the 100-year flood and then reconstructing the buildings. The selected alternative involved relocation of the entire community to a new site outside the flood prone area.

The Arizona legislature facilitated this in 1979 by passing a law permitting state land to be traded for private land. Here was government using its power the way it should. The project was economically justified with $1.40 in benefits for each dollar invested. The solution was socially responsible since the entire community was relocated. The land would be allowed to revert to the natural condition of the existing floodplain so the environmental impacts were actually positive.

The Corps of Engineers used its authority under the 1948 Flood Control Act to act swiftly, since the law permitted it to bypass the lengthy process of authorizing projects. The Federal expenditure under this law is limited to $3 million and the project was estimated to cost almost $5 million. The State of Arizona cooperated fully and agreed to make up the difference. Additionally, as frosting on the cake, almost $1 million of the projects cost will be repaid over time through sales of the new homes.

Such admirable solutions, regrettably, are all too rare. In the past, governmental entities have relied on structural solutions such as dams, channels, and levees. Another flooded community, Holly Acres, provides a good example of governmental ineptness in solving flood problems. This community is upstream of Allenville about 15 miles closer to Phoenix. In 1965, 8 years before the floodplain law was passed, the county flood control engineer recommended against approval of the subdivision because "it lies entirely within the floodplain. . . ." He also noted that "Damage will occur from any major flood."

The county supervisors unanimously approved the subdivision of J. Holly Smith. The lots were then sold for homes, which were flooded in 1978-80. In May 1979 the Corps of Engineers estimated it would cost less than $5 million to relocate Holly Acres, but only 80 cents in benefits would be realized for each dollar invested. Other alternatives were not seriously considered as the plight of Holly Acres was used to promote Orme Dam.

After the February 1980 flood, the state's largest newspaper, the *Arizona Republic*, sent Mr. and Mrs. Smith of Holly Acres to Washington to tell Congress about the plight of Holly Acres and the need for flood control. In a follow-up editorial the paper flatly stated that "they didn't build in a floodplain" and diagnosed the cause of the flood as the blocking of the channel by debris.

A channel was cleared in the Holly Acres vicinity, but this, unfortunately, will have little effect in large floods. In 1984, therefore, construction began on dikes at a projected cost of $1.2 million. But these, too, are not adequate to provide protection from the sort of flooding that occurred in 1980 unless some form of additional upstream flood control is provided. And so, oddly enough, we are back to the "need" for Orme Dam or "a suitable alternative".

21. Counterattack: The Eagles

Orme Dam was obviously not dead but only asleep. Arizona's largest newspaper began a campaign to get its readers to clip a coupon and send it to their congressperson, asking for Orme to be built. The new governor, Bruce Babbitt, appointed a new committee to study the dam and its alternatives. The 28-member group included two Fort McDowell residents and the head of the local Audubon Society. The other members were predominantly in favor of Orme Dam.

Committee members were provided with reams of information, but only the government's side was presented. The committee in general did not seem to be too interested in facts anyway, but they were concerned about the possibility that national publicity over the Indians and the destruction of a bald eagle habitat would scare Congress away from funding Orme. Of even greater concern was the threat of a lawsuit that would delay the dam's construction indefinitely. The CAP legislation seemed to preclude a lawsuit by the Yavapai tribe. Congress had provided that their land could be condemned if they refused the monetary offer. Litigation was possible concerning the numerous archaeological sites in the Orme reservoir area, but with enough money these could be excavated while the dam was being built.

The bald eagle, however, was the point of greatest vulnerability to a lawsuit, and the Audubon Society was pre-

pared to go all the way to the U.S. Supreme Court to protect
this endangered species. They had a potentially powerful
case since our national symbol is protected by at least three
federal laws: the Bald Eagle Act of 1940, the Migratory
Bird Treaty Act, and the Endangered Species Act.

The society had considered using the Endangered Species
Act in its 1975 lawsuit over elimination of alternatives to
Orme Dam. The species that was in jeopardy in that case
was the Yuma clapper rail, which nested in the marshes at
the confluence of the Salt and Verde rivers. But this rather
nondescript bird would have excited little public interest.
Also there was a fair population of the birds along the
Colorado River. The local Audubon Society decided not to
risk using the Endangered Species Act in a weak case.

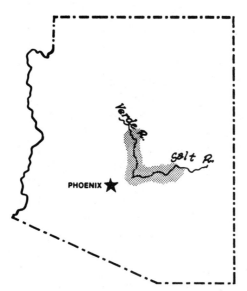

Fig. 44 Breeding range of
Arizona's bald eagles.
Maricopa Audubon Society.

The bald eagle is a magnificent bird whose numbers have
severely declined because of DDT pollution, shooting and
other man-made hazards. The larger northern species is
still plentiful in Alaska, but the southern subspecies of our
national symbol has been particularly depleted. There were
only 7 successful nesting territories in the entire southwestern United States. Three of these would be inundated by

Orme. More than half of the young eaglets produced in Arizona each year came from these areas.

It certainly seemed that the Endangered Species Act was ready-made for a situation like this, especially since Orme Dam's economic justification was questionable. The local Audubon Society suffered some anxious moments, however, when a lawsuit was filed over Tellico Dam. Here the economics were as bad, if not worse than Orme's. The Tellico Dam was 90% complete, and its builder, the Tennessee Valley Authority, admitted it would not be economically justifiable to complete the remaining 10%. In spite of this, local interests pushed Congress to complete the project. The Endangered Species Act was invoked to protect a small fish, the snail darter, which was even more nondescript than the Yuma clapper rail. Phoenix Auduboners were afraid the Tellico case might endanger the Endangered Species Act.

It would have been infinitely more desirable to have a spectacular species like the bald eagle test the Endangered Species Act. There is a well-worn legal premise that bad facts make bad law, and the Tellico Dam's snail darter presented pretty bad facts to Congress. Probably the only species that could have provided worse facts was an herbaceous plant called the furbish louseworth. Tellico Dam was completed, and the Endangered Species Act was amended, but fortunately not repealed.

It is a sad commentary upon our society that it cannot yet comprehend the significance of eliminating even the most minute species from our world. Even from a purely pragmatic perspective, it does not make sense. The armadillo is the only animal that contracts leprosy and could help in its cure. Tree shrews have recently become considered ideal in research on human sexuality. The lowly sea squirt may be the source of new drugs against cancer, the common cold, flu, and herpes. Seaweed is now being processed for everything from birth control to prevention of ulcers and venereal symptoms.

The day may yet come when "critters" are appreciated for purely aesthetic reasons. Meanwhile the economist tries to evaluate the monetary loss of eliminating them. We know that the public is willing to pay for pet fish, birds, and even reptiles and amphibians. Native plants, especially cacti, also have a monetary value. It is more difficult to evaluate the last members of a species in monetary terms, especially since their sale is illegal. They are rather like rare works of art, and the art auction of the endangered species is the political arena.

America is aware of the Audubon Society's successful efforts to save the egret and the whooping crane. Today the society is involved in all aspects of the environment, from energy and water to eagles and whales. The Phoenix group, known as the Maricopa Audubon Society, was most concerned about the destruction of the last rivers in Arizona. Reclamation projects have eliminated many of southern Arizona's free flowing rivers, some of which were heavily forested with mesquite and cottonwood trees. The CAP and its four dams would destroy most of the remaining portions of this valuable riparian habitat. One of these dams, Hooker, which is just across the Arizona border in New Mexico, would inundate portions of the first wilderness area set aside by Congress. This particularly incensed the Sierra Club and the Friends of the Earth.

The 25 miles of river that Orme would flood contains the highest concentration of non-colonial nesting birds in the entire United States. In addition, a colony of hundreds of great blue herons lives there. Dr. Witzeman, a Phoenix anesthesiologist and president of the Maricopa Audubon Society, did a masterful job of informing conservationists in the Southwest and the nation of these facts—and raising funds to hire experts and to prepare for a lawsuit. The powerful National Wildlife Federation, with its array of legal, environmental and resource experts, soon joined the battle, primarily to save the bald eagle.

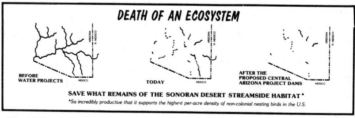

Fig. 45 The destruction of Arizona's streamside habitat. *Maricopa Audubon Society.*

Typically, the Bureau of Reclamation, with billions of U.S. tax dollars behind them, attempted to hire the best experts to prove its point of view. The bureau realized that it might have to defend its decisions in court, since the Audubon Society's 400,000 national membership is quite dedicated and contains the real eagle experts.

The battle raged on in numerous committee meetings, public hearings, and in the local news media. The bureau first argued that the eagles could utilize the lake that would be created by Orme Dam. The society countered by noting that none of these southwestern eagles nest along the existing reservoirs. The principal reason seems to be the lack of trees along the lake shores. The eagles need perches from which to hunt for their major food, which is fish. The fluctuating water levels of desert reservoirs, due to the summer irrigation, preclude the growth of trees. This blunted the bureau's argument that northern bald eagles nest along lakes.

The bureau then decided it could construct artificial hunting perches along the shores of existing reservoirs and build a series of shallow channels more than two miles long in order to mitigate the loss of eagle habitat. Audubon retorted by noting that the bureau might as well put the eagles in zoos. They added that the best mitigation would be to keep the flowing rivers as they are.

Finally the bureau argued that the eagles would soon disappear from these rivers so near to the burgeoning Phoenix area, since they surely could not withstand the disturbance caused by thousands of people tubing down the river. Audubon pointed out that this population began nesting in the winter and by the time the summer crowds arrived, the young had been fledged.

There was little doubt that Orme opponents would file lawsuits if the government tried to build the dam. The national publicity from such a suit was itself a threat. It was not difficult to envision Hiawatha Hood, chairman of the Yavapai tribe, and Dr. Witzeman of the Audubon Society, on national TV shows. The government's flooding of Indians and eagles was certainly a saleable commodity. Combined with the taxpayer issue, it could threaten the CAP as well as Orme Dam.

And adverse publicity was mounting in the national news media. A coalition of more than 20 local and national groups was formed to support the Fort McDowell community in its opposition to Orme Dam. It covered the political spectrum from the far left to the far right and included powerful environmental and Indian groups and church groups of almost every major denomination. A high U.S. Interior Department official called it the most effective coalition ever put together to oppose a dam construction project.

Table 7: Some Organizations Opposing Orme Dam

American Civil Liberties Union
Arizona Democratic Party (1978 Platform)
Arizona Ecumenical Council
Arizona Libertarian Party
Catholic Diocese of Phoenix/Human Development Council
Citizens Concerned About the Project
Committee to Save Ft. McDowell Indian Community
Construction, Production & Maintenance Labors Union
      Local No. 383
Friends Committee on National Legislation
Friends Meeting of Phoenix/Tempe
Friends of the Earth
Inter-tribal Councils of Arizona and New Mexico
Maricopa Audubon Society
National Audubon Society
National Indian Lutheran Board
National Wildlife Federation
Phoenix Gray Panthers
Presbytery of the Grand Canyon
Salt River Pima-Maricopa Indian Community
Sierra Club
Tempe Democrats
Valley Republicans

Yet only a short time before, these groups had hardly heard of Orme Dam. If they had, they had been told it was needed for water supply for this arid land or to protect the area from devastating floods. They were, however, concerned about the destruction of the homes of human beings or animals, the waste of tax dollars, or just plain aesthetics. When their interests led them to investigate the issue and they found that Orme wasn't *needed* if the existing facilities were operated intelligently, the individual groups coalesced into an effective coalition that could potentially obviate the need for a lawsuit.

Meanwhile the price of Orme was escalating astronomically. When authorized in 1968 it was estimated to cost $38 million. This rose to $229 million in 1977, than tripled to $700 million in 1981. This created potential cost over-run problems for the entire CAP, with the possibility that Congress would have to reauthorize the entire package, reopening the Pandora's box that had been so quickly shut in 1977.

The last price increase was even more significant. Orme's 1980 price tag of $350 million had doubled in just one year. This surely indicated a major design change. Exploration of *this* issue turned out to be earthshaking, for the Orme Dam of the 1970s, an engineering analysis revealed, would have been an unsafe structure!

" . . .and this is our latest model."

Fig. 46 *Dave Campbell.*

22. The Noah Flood and Alternatives

At 11:57 A.M. on June 5, 1976, Teton Dam, a 305-foot high earthfill structure on the Teton River in Madison County, Idaho, failed and released the contents of its reservoir. The dam had just been completed and was being filled for the first time. It was designed by the Bureau of Reclamation. Eleven deaths and more than $400 million in damages resulted from this disaster.

The story behind the construction of this dam is rather shocking. It has been succinctly summarized in the paper by University of Utah economists:

So intent on constructing the project were the "water hustlers" from the Bureau and from local and state groups, that the inferior and unstable site characteristics were essentially ignored, although the site was grouted an unusual three times. A benefit-cost analysis done today (after the failure) would be rather devastating.

Yet, as we will see, the bureau has attempted to use this disaster to get hundreds of millions of tax dollars into its coffers and even to build new dams.

Following the disastrous collapse of the Teton Dam, the Interior Department funded a study by a National Academy of Sciences committee of professional engineers. It cited deficiencies in the bureau's dam safety program, noting that responsibility is spread throughout the sprawling agency and adding that "Responsibilities are so diffused . . . that satisfactory execution is dependent upon informal cooperation and communication among the bureau's staff."

When this report was released late in 1977, the bureau also released its internal report listing 17 unsafe dams. Two of these, Roosevelt and Stewart Mountain, are on the Salt River upstream from Phoenix. A spokesman for the Salt River Project, however, said their dams "are 100 percent safe."

In February 1979 a spokesman for Citizens Concerned About the Project informed the Arizona legislature that the bureau's report stated that "Roosevelt Dam would fail" in the event of a maximum probable flood, and that: "Under present operating restrictions, the normal water level in the reservoir has been reduced to protect against failure during intermediate floods." SRP discounted these warnings, according to newspaper reports, and accused CCAP of "manipulation on the part of special interest." The bureau's Arizona spokesman also told the news media that the Salt River Project's dams were safe.

Roosevelt is the largest dam on the SRP system, with a capacity of 1,300,000 acre feet. A Freedom of Information Act request to the bureau's Washington office in mid-1979 resulted in a statement that it would not fail but that Stewart Mountain Dam downstream could fail. The 1977 report had included Stewart Mountain but had said it would not fail. This is the closest dam to the Phoenix area, only 25 miles upstream from the beginning of the populated area.

The bureau concluded that the dam would be fine so long as flows did not exceed 105,000 cubic feet per second (cfs). However, the three upstream dams have spillways that will pass 150,000 cfs. Roosevelt Dam's spillway can be controlled to reduce the release to 105,000 cfs but water would begin backing up behind that dam, overtopping it. Sustained overtopping would erode the face and foundation of the dam and it could fail.

In February 1980, in the middle of the flood, Governor Bruce Babbitt announced that Stewart Mountain Dam was in danger of failure and residents should be prepared to evacuate!

The reason the disaster did not occur is that the flood peaked before its flow exceeded the capacity of the dam's spillway. If the floodwaters had continued to rise, the dam would have been overtopped, eroding its foundation. According to the bureau, this "could cause failure of the dam."

To understand the dynamics of the situation, think of your bathroom sink or tub. There is an outlet near the top to prevent overtopping in case the inflow from the faucet is too great. The spillway is essentially an opening in the dam which is lower than the top of the structure. Floodwaters are passed through so overtoppping does not occur—unless the floodflows exceed the spillway's capacity.

Dams, of course, are designed not to fail. In order to prevent the structure from being overtopped, the spillway is generally designed to safely pass the maximum "probable" flood. This is the largest flood that can "reasonably" be expected to occur. It is generally too large to be controlled by the dam from the standpoint of economic feasibility so it is passed through the spillway to protect the integrity of the dam structure. There is also a maximum "possible" flood, which is the largest event that can "theoretically" be expected to occur. Then of course there is the Noah flood.

Prior to the three events of 1978-80, the maximum probable flood that was expected to flow into Roosevelt Lake was 214,000 cfs. This was subsquently raised to 680,000 cfs, apparently due to the new statistical data available. Reportedly, the Corps of Engineers had been arguing for a larger design flow for years. The Teton disaster and the trilogy of floods apparently convinced the bureau that the corps was right.

The maximum flow on the Verde River was raised from 237,000 cfs to 760,000 cfs. These new flows had a tremendous impact on the proposed Orme Dam, which had been designed to pass a peak flow of only 336,000 cfs. Since it was designed as an earthern dam, it surely would fail and the Phoenix area would thus sustain a truly major catastrophe.

To permit such a large flow to pass without overtopping the dam requires a tremendous increase in the size of the spillway. Spillways are usually constructed of concrete, which is much more expensive than the earthen dam itself. This explains the huge increase in Orme's price tag.

One of the reasons for the large inflow to the Orme Dam site would be the presumed failure of Stewart Mountain

Dam, which is less than 10 miles upstream on the Salt River. In addition, the three dams further upstream would be overtopped by 12 to 23 feet of water. These dams were not designed to be overtopped so this condition must be considered serious. Failure hinges upon duration of overtopping and the construction of the structures.

This could all be prevented by raising Roosevelt Dam to prevent its being overtopped. This was recommended as far back as 1970 since it would kill two birds with one stone by reducing the flow into Stewart Mountain Dam. The greater enlargement proposed in 1981 for Roosevelt would cost approximately $125 million, with an additional $33 million required for Stewart Mountain.

This would also reduce the maximum flood into Orme to less than one million cubic feet per second, considerably reducing the cost of Orme. Obviously the cost could be reduced even further if flows from the Verde River could be similarly reduced. Sure enough, the two dams on that river, the Horseshoe and Bartlett Dams, were also declared unsafe—and thus the Cliff Dam entered the scene.

Cliff would be built between the two dams, at a cost of more than 200 million dollars. It would reduce flows sufficiently to let the design flow pass safely through the spillway

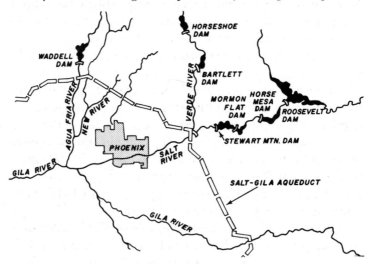

Fig. 47 Rivers and dams in the Phoenix area. *U.S. Bureau of Reclamation.*

of the downstream dam, Bartlett. It would reduce the design flow at Orme to only 270,000 cfs, less than Orme's original spillway design. Accordingly it would reduce Orme's cost to $328 million, less than its 1980 price tag—but the problems of the Indians, eagles and inner tubers remained.

Accordingly, the bureau looked for alternative sites for regulatory storage, which is Orme Dam's primary function as we noted before. Waddell Dam is on the Agua Fria River northwest of Phoenix and is close to the CAP aqueduct. Raising the dam to provide increased storage for CAP water was the least costly alternative but the bureau's major criterion seems to be "the more the merrier." To illustrate, suppose the government could spend $10 to get $20 in benefits, or could spend $100 to get $120 in benefits. Both projects are cost-effective because their benefit/cost ratios are greater than 1.0 (2.0 and 1.2 respectively). The government would choose the latter because it returns $20 in net benefits while the former returns only $10.

The private sector would use the $100 to invest in ten $10 projects to get $100 in net benefits. This is the reason that the government is required to do an economic analysis—to select the most cost-effective projects from the multitude of choices around the nation. In this case the government rejected the raising of the existing dam in favor of building a whole new structure at the same site in order to get more storage—at a cost of $284 million.

Another seemingly cost-effective method rejected was the use of groundwater recharge to store excess CAP water. This appeared to coincide with the supposed purpose of the CAP—to reduce the groundwater mining. The maximum regulatory storage capacity provided under any of the alternatives was 500,000 acre feet (af), while the annual mining of groundwater in central Arizona exceeds 1,500,000 af. It would be possible to simply replace the water that was mined during the peak summer period with CAP water pumped into central Arizona in the winter.

It would be a simple matter to release CAP water from its canal into the dry river beds of the Salt, Aqua Fria, Gila and other rivers and streams of central Arizona that have suitable soil structures. For example, a 1968 report by the leading water engineering firm in the southwest stated that "an estimated 95% recharge will take place" in the Salt River Channel. This is more efficient than storage in reservoirs, where evaporation takes its toll.

This concept is particularly adaptable to the uncertainty of the flows in the Colorado River. Its capacity would be large enough to handle even the highest runoff years of record. After considerable prodding by Orme Dam opponents, the bureau agreed to investigate recharging CAP water into the Salt River. The bureau did all it could to denigrate this concept. First it said not enough was known about the recharge capability of central Arizona's watercourses. The Salt River Project held a groundwater recharge symposium in 1978 and, one by one, Arizona speakers said it could not be done. Then, one by one, speakers from California to Texas said they had been doing it for years.

Meanwhile in northeastern Colorado, farmers were recharging their aquifers in the winter for use during the high demand summer season. They had plans to increase substantially this wise practice — but the bureau has plans to obviate even the present practice by building Narrows Dam. Recharged water would cost $2/af while the Bureau's plan would cost $135/af.

In one of its more blatant maneuvers, the bureau evaluated the recharge alternative at 6⅝% while using a 3½% discount rate for the dam. Small wonder that they found their dam more justifiable! An analysis of Narrows Dam by University of Montana economics professor Thomas Power found it would return only 15 cents for each dollar invested.

Back in Arizona, the trilogy of floods in the late 1970s reaffirmed the recharge capabilility of the Salt River bed. It was estimated that as much as 50% of the releases recharged to the underground reservoir. Much more would have soaked in if the water had not been released in such great quantities. In a small release in 1973, virtually all the water recharged before it left the Phoenix area.

The bureau then proceeded to make this alternative as expensive as possible. They added all kinds of hardware, from stilling basins to pumps. They simply refused to follow

Mother Nature's example, and the Phoenix area lost an inexpensive and potentially aesthetic alternative. Small amounts of water could have been released continually from the CAP aqueduct to recharge both the underground reservoir and a series of small lakes. The latter would provide recreation where the people are, in the heart of the Phoenix area, and could bring north and south Phoenix together. The dry river bed has always been considered an eyesore and a dividing line—like railroad tracks in so many towns. The lakes could be surrounded with ball courts, picnic areas, shady trees, or just plain open space where kids could catch lizards and frogs and collect pet rocks. The concept for such a park project was conceived in the 1960s and is generally referred to as the "Rio Salado" Project, after the spanish name for the Salt River.

Alternatively, CAP water would be released into other watercourses, giving the Salt River bed a chance to dry out to improve its recharge ability, but the lakes would still provide recreation. Streams that have not flowed for almost a century could be restored, at least during the winter. Few realize that Arizona was full of flowing streams before cattle overgrazed the watersheds prior to the turn of the century. Where today there is desert, the grass was at least as high as an antelope's eye. It should here be noted that University of Arizona scientists contend that restoring this grassland could provide much more water than the CAP.

The government offered four non-Orme alternatives, all of which included Cliff Dam. This is the type of "planning" which led the Director of the California Department of Water Resources to make the following observation in 1980:

"The scope of the federal government's water planning efforts remains too single-purposed . . . When general planning studies are made that offer such solutions as reclamation, groundwater storage, or other innovative means for solving problems, the studies tend to be ignored because they do not focus on specified dam projects."

The bureau's "preferred" alternative provided virtually the same regulatory storage and flood control as Orme. It consisted of building a new Waddell dam for storage, constructing Cliff Dam and the maximum raising or reconstructing of Roosevelt Dam.

The Ft. McDowell tribe accepted this alternative because it would not flood their homeland. Audubon and other conservation and environmental groups opposed it because it included Cliff Dam, which would flood an additional 6 miles of scarce riverine habitat that is utilized by two pairs of nesting bald eagles. CCAP questioned its exorbitant and unnecessary cost.

Plan 6: New Waddell + Cliff + Roosevelt + Reconstructed Stewart Mtn. Dam

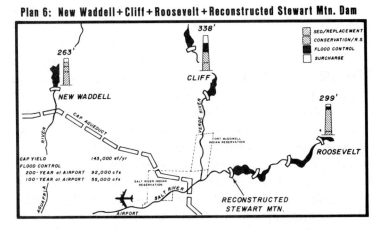

Fig. 48 The proposed alternative to Orme Dam. *U.S. Bureau of Reclamation.*

23. The Battle Over Dam Safety

The total cost of the bureau's new plan, Plan 6, was $746 million. Its implementation would mean that the CAP had exceeded its cost ceiling and would have to go back to Congress for reauthorization. Rather than take this risky route, the bureau found another method to finance a substantial portion of the cost. Two years after the Teton disaster, Congress passed the Reclamation Safety of Dams Act and authorized $100 million to repair unsafe dams. This was only adequate for Stewart Mountain Dam repairs, so in the early 1980s amendments were introduced to increase the authorized amount to $750 million. Fully $350 million of this was slated for Arizona. The big question is whether this money can be used to build Cliff Dam—and whether the dam is needed.

Government studies have indicated that Bartlett and the four Salt River dams are unsafe not only during the maximum probable flood but also during the maximum credible earthquake. Since Cliff would be built upstream of Bartlett it would have no effect on this type of failure. During the maximum flood, however, Bartlett Dam would be overtopped and potentially fail. In fact, Bartlett would be overtopped during the 1,000 year flood, but since it is a concrete dam, failure would not be expected.

The bureau in a June 1981 memorandum report noted that the maximum flood could be passed safely around Bartlett by improving its spillway and raising the dam. The cost would range from \$85 to \$97.5 million. A study by a private consulting engineering firm commissioned by the Corps of Engineers showed that Bartlett could be made safe for less than \$11 million by the construction of another spillway near the dam. The bureau simply said auxiliary spillways of this magnitude "are not used," even though the Corps has used them on its Mississippi River levee system.

Horseshoe Dam is upstream from both Bartlett and the proposed Cliff Dam. If the latter is built, Horseshoe would be breached and innundated by Cliff's reservoir, thereby eliminating any safety problems. According to the aforementioned private consultant's report, Horseshoe could be made safe for \$54 million. The bureau's study placed the cost at \$125 million. Since Horseshoe is an earthen dam, it is assumed to fail if it is overtopped—but it would take a flood that would occur once every 3,000 years to overtop it! When informed of this, a Phoenix engineer quipped: "Next we'll provide protection from meteors." Surely there are more important needs in our nation, especially in light of the deficit.

This brings us to a major philosophical question: when is a dam safe? California's Auburn dam, upstream from Sacramento, was designed to withstand a 5.5 earthquake. In 1979 a state advisory panel effectively vetoed its construction by pointing out that it was to be built on a major fault and should be able to withstand a much higher magnitude earthquake. This is quite fortunate since Dr. Duffield, a colleague of Dr. Power at the University of Montana, did an economic analysis of Auburn which showed that the bureau's 1.72 benefit-cost ratio really should be reduced to 0.28 at a $6\frac{5}{8}\%$ discount rate.

The evaluation of dam safety was the topic of an American Society of Civil Engineers conference in the winter of 1976, shortly after the Teton Dam disaster. It was pointed out that the Corps of Engineers probable maximum flood had a recurrence interval of 10,000 years, which is a conservative estimate with essentially a zero probability of occurrence. The conference was told that the risk cost should be balanced against the safety cost. Flood forecasting and warning and

emergency evacuation were offered as a means of circum-
venting human values. The conference was also told: ". . .
occasional temporary evacuation, upon warning at potentially endangered areas *which can be identified* in the dam
safety program, seems like a viable alternative to a national
cost of millions of dollars to make dams *unnecessarily* safe."

Obviously the 685-foot-high Auburn Dam, only 40 miles
from Sacramento, should be made as safe as possible if it
is built. The 300-foot-high proposed Cliff Dam is less than
50 miles upstream from Phoenix. Its 1,650,000 acre-foot
storage capacity would make it the largest dam on the Salt
and Verde River system, and it surely should be made safe.
But Horseshoe Dam has a storage capacity of only 142,830
acre feet and is more than 50 miles upstream of Phoenix.
There would be ample warning time in the event of a 3,000-
year flood, so loss of life would appear improbable. Risk
analysis should be used to determine whether the damages
resulting from failure would be worth the cost of modifying
the dam. This is standard practice in the design of highway
bridges. The bureau did not do a risk analysis, in spite of
the urging of the Professional Engineering Society in
Phoenix.

In April 1983, 7 years after the release of the first Draft
Environmental Impact Statement (DEIS) on Orme Dam,
the bureau released the DEIS on Orme Alternatives. Orme
opponents immediately pointed out that no alternatives
were considered for Cliff Dam. Since the National Environmental Policy Act, which was passed during the Nixon Administration, requires the consideration of alternatives, the
Final EIS was released in February 1984 with an additional
alternative.

The new alternative consisted of the aforementioned repairs to the Verde River dams. Its cost was $47 million less
than Plan 6, whose price tag had escalated to the billion
dollar mark. The benefit-cost ratios of both plans were almost identical (1.84 for Plan 6 vs. 1.74), but Plan 6 had
$11 million more in net economic benefits ($71 vs. $60
million). Apparently based upon this type of analysis by
the bureau, the Secretary of Interior chose Plan 6 as the
alternative to Orme Dam.

Cliff Dam is the reason Plan 6 has more net benefits. The Bureau reasoned that, since Congress mandated making the dams safe, Cliff Dam is per se justified and assumed its benefit-cost ratio was 1:1. It then incrementally enlarged Cliff to provide water storage, flood control, etc. The bureau added 29 feet to the 260-foot-high dam that was designed solely for dam safety purposes. The increased cost of $47 million was a fraction of the cost of constructing a new dam for water supply, flood control, etc.

But are these benefits legitimate? Earlier we discussed the way the bureau computes benefits for water supply. Let us now take a look at their flood control benefits. Most Americans assume that these benefits result from the protection of existing residents from inundation, but this accounts for only 40% of Cliff's flood control benefits. The rest, which account for a fifth of Cliff's total benefits, are known as "location" benefits. This was formerly known as land enhancement.

Plan 6 and most of the other alternatives would reduce the 100-year flood flow from 215,000 cubic feet per second (cfs) to 55,000 cfs. The land that would be "rescued" from the floodplain could then be developed without restraint. This is the "Rio Salado Project" selected by the Rio Salado Development District, which was created by the state legislature. It would require the relocation of 300 low income families, mostly Mexican Americans, and would cost Arizona taxpayers $696 million dollars to develop, not in-

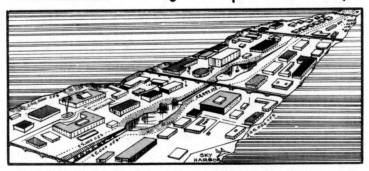

Fig. 49 The Salt River floodplain if upstreams dams are built. *Maricopa Audubon Society.*

WITHOUT CLIFF DAM: Using a floodplain - Common sense style

Fig. 50 The Salt River floodplain without upstream dams. *Maricopa Audubon Society.*

cluding the cost of Cliff Dam. As one of the district's directors noted, the Rio Salado Project is the only remaining reason for building Cliff (or Orme) Dam. Should U.S. tax dollars be used to permit commercial development of the floodplain in Phoenix?

Without Plan 6, the floodplain could be open space and greenbelt, as suggested by the local Audubon Society. A study commissioned by the Rio Salado Development District found that a Rio Salado Project could be developed without additional upstream dams at a cost of only $71 million. It would include a lake and parks already planned by the City of Tempe and would provide protection for existing homes within the floodplain. It is essentially a "nonstructural" solution, and it would appear that federal funding could be used to help develop it instead of Orme or Cliff Dam.

In 1974 Congress passed a law requiring consideration of:

. . . nonstructural alternatives to prevent or reduce flood damages including, but not limited to, floodproofing of structures; floodplain regulation; acquisition of floodplain lands for recreational, fish and wildlife, and other public purposes; and relocation with a view toward formulating the most economically, socially, and environmentally acceptable means of reducing or preventing flood damages.

Here was the perfect opportunity to implement the law, but recalcitrant bureaucrats refused to even quote the above section in their reports.

A similar situation existed in Scottsdale, Arizona, in the early '70s. The Corps of Engineers wanted to build a concrete flood control channel through the heart of the town, but the citizenry fought for the greenbelt approach. The National Society of Professional Engineers selected Scottsdale's Indian Bend Wash Greenbelt Flood Control Project as one of the ten outstanding Engineering Achievements for 1978.

The 1974 law should have made it even easier to implement such an alternative along the Salt River through Phoenix. Additionally, in 1973 Arizona had also passed a floodplain law which prohibited construction in a floodway. It was possible to build structures within the 100-year floodplain, but the added cost of raising the floor levels of buildings above the flood levels depressed the value of this land. It certainly seemed feasible to use flood control funds to acquire some of these less costly lands for "recreational, fish and wildlife, and other public purposes." Combined with the Tempe Rio Salado plan and the gradual development of parks by local governments, this nonstructural flood control plan could create 40 miles of open space through the heart of Phoenix.

But the decision makers had long ago decided that 50,000 cfs was the only floodplain they would accept. They even balked at the possibility of a 55,000 cfs flow. Their plan was to buy the floodplain land while its price was depressed, then sell or lease it to developers after the upstream dams protected it. They claimed Cliff Dam was necessary to implement their Rio Salado. The bureau's 1983 DEIS even stated: "A Tempe Rio Salado Project would be implemented. The overall Rio Salado concept was assumed not to be developed because it is dependent upon upstream flood control." Yet only a few months earlier a report for the Rio Salado Development District, prepared by a Boston consultant, showed that the overall Rio Salado could be implemented without upstream dams. It would cost $565 million to develop the lakes, roads, etc. while the fancier version would cost $696 million plus the cost of Cliff. The Tempe project, which is similar to the nonstructural plan discussed earlier with the addition of lakes and levees, would cost $71 million. This is a far cry from the Flood Plain Management plan considered in Orme's first DEIS in 1976, which stated:

This nonstructural flood control alternative would require the acquisition evacuation and zoning of 102,000 acres of floodplain lands and their exclusion from further infringement by various economic interests . . . The cost of such a plan is estimated at $1,170,000,000 . . .

In light of Arizona's 1973 floodplain law, one must wonder why the bureau felt it was necessary to buy the land (unless it was to make this option look too expensive). The bureau also mentioned the Rio Salado in this DEIS:

. . . It is viewed with favor by many residents of the Salt River Valley. However, in 1974 a bond election was defeated for funds to purchase some of the required right-of-way. This potential project is predicated on upstream flood control.

Thus while admitting that a Rio Salado Project predicated upon upstream flood control was rejected by Phoenix voters, the bureau continues to use Rio Salado to push for upstream controls.

As noted in the beginning of this chapter, the bureau hopes to finance much of the cost of Cliff Dam through the 1978 Safety of Dams (SOD) Act. This appears rather doubtful since that act covers modifications to existing dams, not new dams like Cliff. A 1983 amendment to the SOD Act which would have permitted construction of new dams failed to get out of Congress. The act also appears to require "least cost" solutions to safety problems. In its July 1981 Memorandum Report, the bureau estimated the cost of modifying the existing Verde dams at $210 million and Cliff's cost at only $193 million. They therefore selected Cliff Dam. Yet only three months later, the bureau's "Factbook" listed Cliff's cost at $241 million. The least cost solution would consist of constructing an auxiliary spillway at Bartlett for less than $11 million.

Even the Bureau's tremendous increase in the sizing of the maximum probable flood has been questioned — not by Orme opponents but by Arizona's largest energy utility. In a reported attempt to resurrect Orme by reducing the size of the spillway, Arizona Public Service selected the same consulting engineer who had worked with Melvin Belli on the SRP lawsuit. That water resource specialist concluded that the maximum flood should be only two-thirds the size computed by the bureau. He noted that the bureau's maximum flood was greater than the great floods on the Colorado River and almost as large as the peak flow of the Mississippi River at St. Louis.

The final chapter on Orme and its alternatives has yet to be written. At least one Arizona congressman continues to push for Orme. By 1984 the bald eagle nesting territories in Arizona had increased to 15. A new nest was discovered just upstream from the new Waddell Dam site and another nest was found right in the middle of the proposed Cliff reservoir. Mrs. Carolina Castillo Butler has become a director of CCAP and has begun educating her fellow Mexican Americans who live along the route of the proposed Rio Salado Project. Opposition to that project has begun to emerge and early in 1984 the Arizona legislature shelved the proposed plan for its financing. Congress finally passed the Safety of Dams bill, but without the provisions permitting new dams.

"Never mind the cost, we want to build another dam."

Fig. 51 *Dave Campbell.*

Conclusion: The American Way

In October 1982, when it appeared that Orme Dam had been stopped, a local Arizona newspaper carried the headline "Orme Proves Little People Can Win." Clearly we have a long way to go towards achieving our national identity as a democratic republic when the will of the people is described as "winning." This nation "of the people, by the people and for the people" has become a nation of the politicians, by the bureaucrats and for the profit of a few.

America has always been considered the land of the rugged individual. Private enterprise was the way we solved most of our problems. Local government built streets and water systems. As Alexander Hamilton noted in the *Federalist Papers*, the principal reason for the establishment of the federal government was national defense.

Washington politicans then decided that the best way to assure re-election was by doing favors for their constituents. This was originally rationalized by claiming that local governments were not able to solve their problems without help from the federal government. Flood control is a good example. Congress agreed to pay half the cost, thus getting its foot in the door. Within a few years the politicians walked in the rest of the way with full federal funding. The resulting dam building spree led Will Rogers to make the following observation about politicans back in 1933:

Say, have you noticed that they are always wanting the government to spend the taxpayers' money to build something? This

dam business is getting to be quite a racket. Every congressman, if he's got a little stream running through his client's pasture, wants to get an appropriation to dam it up with federal funds, generally under a racket called "Flood Control."
If the politicians have their way, there won't be a foot of water in this country that's not standing above a dam.

The bureaucrats working for so-called construction agencies like the Bureau of Reclamation and the Corps of Engineers have been more than willing to help the politicans justify the spending of tax dollars. This is because their very jobs often depend upon finding new projects to build. Equally important is the pressure put on bureaucrats to build projects in order to achieve advancement within the agency.

The author's experience as an engineer with the Corps of Engineers provides a good example of this pressure. His analysis of seven different flood control projects showed that none of them were economically justified. In the worst case the flood problem was caused by the mayor of the community, who had filled in a necessary ponding area in order to build apartments. The local community was actually asking the federal taxpayer to solve a problem created by their own chief official.

The engineering and economic analysis turned out to be the least difficult part of the process. The major hurdle was convincing the department head that the projects were not justified. The acceptance of any one of these projects would have led to the hiring of one or more engineers to plan and design the projects. This could have resulted in a higher grade for the department head. Thus the bureaucracy grows and grows, gobbling up tax dollars in the process.

Bureaucracies even seem to have a different concept of economics, as the following quote from the previously cited 1979 article from a professional journal noted. The University of Utah economists observed that the former head of the Bureau of Reclamation

. . . revealed his definition of "economics" to coincide with what most people, laymen or economists, would call profligate spending. To him, economics means using up energy and resources to generate cash flow. If a thing of beauty or utility is created in the process, the environment must also have been improved. Persons unwary enough to suggest that development might have been handled a different way, or who disagree with his criterion, are subject to scathing attack.

Bureaucracies are like vines—they need constant attention to get them to grow the way we want them. They should not be planted unless they are going to be cared for. If a vine has been planted in the wrong place, or is not producing, or has grown out of control, it is sometimes necessary to dig it up by the roots and get rid of it.

The Bureau of Reclamation has grown out of control. The 1902 homestead law which spawned it is no longer viable. That the bureau has not been productive, at least in recent decades, is confirmed by the aforementioned University of Utah economists:

... results of a number of studies of broad social impacts are available (some sponsored by the Bureau of Reclamation itself). They show that post-1950 water investments in the Intermountain West and in the Upper Missouri Basin undertaken by BuRec or COE, have had no statistically significant impact on income per capita, employment, or gross sales, when compared with companion areas that did not enjoy such investments.

The bureau is now a bureaucracy looking for a purpose. Given enough time, it no doubt will find projects to build — and eventually will bring water from Alaska to Arizona. It is time to repeal reclamation. This would result in the elimination of a bureaucracy, a much sought after goal of the Reagan administration. In fact, the lead article in the July 31, 1983, *Arizona Republic* stated:

President Reagon on Saturday called the federal bureaucracy a 'growing administrative monster' and said he will intensify efforts beginning this week to overhaul it and save the equivalent of $2,000 for each American family by 1988.
Renewing his 1980 campaign attacks on 'fraud, waste and abuse,' Reagan said he will call senior appointees to the White House 'to continue an ambitious program to upgrade management of the federal government.'

While the U.S. taxpayer would be the major beneficiary of such a repeal, the vast majority of American farmers would also benefit. They would no longer have to compete in the market place with surplus crops grown with cheap water from giant water projects subsidized by tax dollars — including their own.

Repealing reclamation would also find favor with the environmental community since it would remove the major construction agency from the Department of the Interior. The Bureau of "Wrecklamation," as environmentalists often refer to it, has created conflicts within that department for years.

Most Americans know that the Department of the Interior includes the National Park Service and the U.S. Fish and Wildlife Service. Some are aware that the Bureau of Indian Affairs is also under its wing. Very few realize that the Bureau of Reclamation is in this same department and that its water projects threaten Indian reservations, wildlife areas and endangered species and, in the case of Bridge Canyon (now Hualapai) dams, even Grand Canyon National Park. Its demise would result in the Department of the Interior being primarily devoted to conservation of our natural resources, rather than construction with the resultant destruction.

If for any reason the federal government must remain involved in building water projects, the recommendation of the National Water Commission should be heeded:

Costs . . . should be recovered from identifiable beneficiaries . . . with interest equal to prevailing yield rates on long term U.S. Treasury bonds outstanding at the time of construction.

Other bureaucracies involved in federal water projects, like the Corps of Engineers, have other functions which are still viable. The Corps has been a functioning part of the military since revolutionary days and has a definite role in national defense. But it does need constant attention, and a refurbished Interior Department would be better able to oversee the construction activities of the Corps, which is in the Department of Defense.

The Corps does need a major pruning of its flood control branch. Its involvement in local flood control projects seems to encourage local communities to ignore irresponsible use of the flood plains. If a flood does occur, federal funds will be available for repairs, and people move right back into the flood plain. If the situation gets bad enough, federal funds will be provided to build a dam to prevent future floods.

Arizona's Governor, Bruce Babbitt, made the following statement in the June 1982 *Reader's Digest*: "Congress ought to be worrying about arms control and defense instead of potholes in the street. We might just have both an increased chance of survival and better streets." The same rationale certainly applies to local water problems.

Most Washington politicians are more interested in getting a bigger slice of the federal pie than in reducing the size of the pie. The pie has been baked with the taxpayers' dough, which should be taken out of Washington and put back in the hands of the local bakeries. This would result in many innovative recipes—floodplain zoning, reformed laws and policies, drip irrigation, land leveling, etc. In the long run, this would take a lot less time and money than the tired federal solutions of tax, spend and build.

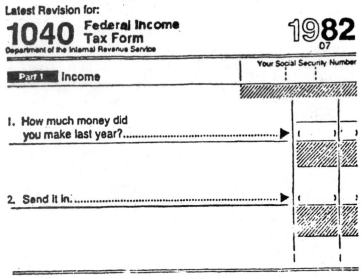

Fig. 52 The tax form of the future? *Devils Advocate, Arizona State University Law School newspaper.*

In the Winter 1982 issue of *Professional Engineer*, an article on "Funding to Meet America's Water Needs" pointed out that in 1957 the federal government funded 10% of state and local public works investment; by the late 1970s, federal financing accounted for over 40% of such expenditures. The article also noted:

In the recent past, when needs were perceived, the easy answer was to seek increased federal financing. This is no longer feasible or desirable. . . . It is a time to reassess priorities, to rebuild the self-sufficiency of local and state revenue systems, and to reestablish a critical working partnership between state and local government and the business and professional communities.

In its January 10, 1983, issue, *Time* magazine noted that the "Repairing of America" will cost hundreds of billions of dollars, with some estimates into the trillions. Hard choices will have to be made, and they can best be made by those who will be directly affected. The *Time* article noted that spending an added $4.3 billion on the roads and bridges most in need of repair would save 17,200 lives and prevent 480,000 personal injuries over the next 15 years. This is not much more than the price tag of the CAP, which the powerful Arizona delegation has managed to get funded every year.

Early in 1984 it was reported that the President's Private Sector Survey on Cost Control listed the CAP as a prime example of congressional pork-barreling. This "Grace Report" chided two thirds of Arizona's congressional delegation for contributing to government waste. In a subsequent column, Donald Lambro of United Features referred to the "rank hyprocrisy of members who denounce undisciplined spending one day, then fight to preserve and extend parochial projects and expenditures the next." The Grace report contended that two of Arizona's congressmen pursued purely parochial interests in fighting attempts to end further funding for the CAP.

The water crisis has been created by the greed of some and the indifference of many. The motivation to overcome this indifference can come from highly charged issues, such as the flooding of Indians and eagles and the wasting of tax dollars in the Orme Dam controversy. Proponents of Orme used the emotionalism of floods and droughts to counter this, but eventually the effect was blunted by educating the public about the facts.

Education can also provide the motivation to overcome indifference. The problem in specialized areas like water, however, is that the expertise lies almost exclusively with those who are employed by the government, either directly or indirectly. Even "private" consultants depend upon government work to sustain them, and the purse strings of state universities are held by the state legislature.

In their efforts to determine the facts, concerned citizens spend their "spare" time wading through mountains of often highly technical reports on topics well outside the scope of their regular full-time jobs. Not infrequently, these people's accuracy is then criticized by bureaucrats who are employed full time as economists, engineers, ecologists, hydrologists, lawyers, etc. and are paid with the tax dollars of the concerned citizens. It is this inequity which initially brought the author into the fray.

The Environmental Impact Statment (EIS) process could provide a solution to this inequity. Originally passed during the Nixon Administration, the National Environmental Policy Act (NEPA) has been criticized for creating a plethora of lawsuits. Yet lost lawsuits are generally the result of the overeagerness on the part of bureaucrats to build projects. As a result, they omit damaging information from the statements and invite lawsuits: the EIS is essentially a disclosure statement and would be impregnable to lawsuits if all the facts were honestly presented. For example, the EIS on Orme could have said that the dam would have flooded Phoenix. While NEPA does not provide a legal remedy for this, one can only imagine the political ramifications of such a disclosure.

Rather than permit the construction agency to prepare the EIS, it would seem wiser to permit those groups that are most likely to protest construction to participate more fully in the preparation of the statement. Possibly they could prepare the EIS themselves, or at least have a say in the selection of consultants who would prepare the EIS. As a result, the groups would be most unlikely to sue and would have access to their own experts. All society would benefit since there would be fewer lawsuits and more fruitful projects.

Hopefully this book has provided sufficient facts to motivate the reader. It has shown that the water crisis is the creation of man, not nature. It is the result of shortcomings in human rules and regulations, not nature's resources. Rather than change their institutions and letting the market place work, local entities have looked to big government to solve their self-imposed crises. Politicians and bureaucrats have been only too willing to exploit the void and further compound the crisis.

This can all be changed by the will of the people, as Orme Dam illustrated on a smaller scale. Although many prominent organizations were visible in the Orme Dam battle, hundreds and even thousands of individuals participated, each in his or her own way. Some contributed money, others volunteered time. Some wrote letters while still others simply called the local office of their senator or representative. This is the way the "little" people won the Orme Dam battle. With the same tactics, they can win the water war.

Appendix

Arizona's Water Supplies

The Hudson Institute uses 2,300,000 acre feet (af) for Arizona's surface water supply and 300,000 af as recharged groundwater. Thus the total renewable supply is 2.6 million af (maf). These are the same figures used in the Arizona Water Commission's Phase II report (2/77).

Of this, 900,000 is from the Colorado River, leaving 1.7 maf for the rest of the state. The U.S. Bureau of Reclamation's 4/75 *Westwide Study* shows 1,793,000 af of surface water in the Gila-Salt subbasin. The Arizona Water Commission's Phase I report (7/75) estimates 1.5 maf as the dependable supply for that area. Virtually all this water would flow into the Phoenix area if not used by others.

Conservatively, then, central Arizona has at least 1.5 maf of renewable water available. There are 325,851 gallons in an acre foot. The following calculation was used to determine the supportable population:

$$\frac{1,500,000 \text{ af x } 325,851 \text{ gallons}}{140 \text{ gal/person/day x } 365 \text{ days}} = 9.5 \text{ million people}$$

The 1/8/82 Arizona Department of Economic Security projection estimates 6,905,000 people in central Arizona (Maricopa, Pima and Pinal Counties) in 2035 A.D..

Arizona Revised Statute 45-141 gives the following priority of water uses: Domestic, municipal, irrigation, stock watering, power and mining uses, and wildlife. Thus it can be argued that domestic uses come first and the cities can use their power of eminent domain to condemn land to acquire water rights. Even if this law is interpreted differently, laws can always be changed and surely would be if population exceeds water supply.

Fair and Geyer (1971) note that: "Ordinarily, 60 to 70% of the total water supplied becomes waste water." Tucson has been reusing approximately 50% of its water. Thus even if central Arizona's population should reach 9 million, there should be more than 700,000 af of wastewater available. This is enough to irrigate 200,000 acres with the current cropping pattern. Only 80,000 acres were in citrus, vegetables, nuts, and fruits in central Arizona in 1980.

The *Westwide Study*, prepared by the Bureau of Reclamation, contains the following statement:

Inasmuch as the water supply available is far in excess of foreseeable demands for municipal and industrial purposes, the justification for such additional imports would have to rely on the value of water for irrigation. It is doubtful if such justification can be demonstrated in the foreseeable future. Thus, it appears that the future water supply of the central Arizona area should be planned on the basis of present water supplies enhanced by whatever additional conservation practices are feasible plus the potential imports from the Central Arizona project.

Yet the bureau contradicts its own study, and relies heavily on municipal and industrial benefits in its economic justification of the CAP.

Water Supplies in other States

The following table shows the amount of water available from surface sources to other states, according to the *Westwide Study*:

Arizona	3,323,000 af
New Mexico	1,940,000
Nevada	4,565,000
Colorado	6,718,000
Platte R. (Denver)	1,841,000
Wyoming	6,616,000
Utah	6,450,000
Salt Lake subbasin	2,640,000
California	50,000,000
South Coastal subbasin	3,550,000

Obviously the oft-repeated statement that most of California's water is in the northern part of the state is true. The more important fact is that the South Coastal basin, which encompasses the Los Angeles-San Diego area, has enough surface water to support 21 million people. Again the bureau admits this in its Westwide Study: ". . . the water supply situation appears generally adequate to meet the midterm projected needs for both major urban and agricultural uses."

The Platte subbasin provides enough surface water to support 10.9 million people. Population projections in the *Westwide Study* indicate that the Denver area will not exceed 5 million until after 2030 A.D..

Water available in the Salt Lake City area can support 15.7 million people, yet the bureau says the area "may experience water shortages in the 1983-1987 time frame" if the Central Utah Project's Bonneville unit is delayed. They do also note that additional M&I water becomes available yearly through "conversion of irrigation uses to M&I purposes." It appears the problem here is quite similar to the Phoenix situation.

In 1980 only 6 states had populations greater than 10 million. These included California (23.6), New York (17.5), Texas (14.2), Pennsylvania (11.8), Illinois (11.4) and Ohio (10.7). In a paper presented at the Seminar on "Development and Population: Alternative Futures in the West" (Colorado State University, August 1-3, 1973), Victor A. Koelzer estimated that the water used by irrigated agriculture in the West could support "up to 50 times the present population, when indirect reuse is considered." Mr. Koelzer, who is Professor of Civil Engineering and Director of the International School of Water Resources Environmental Management at CSU and was a member of the National Water Commission, pointed out that the West could easily absorb the 100 million increase in the nation's population projected for 2000 A.D..

Fair and Geyer's 1971 engineering textbook notes that the national average rate of water use is 150 gallons per person per day. This is the rate used by the Arizona Water Commission in its 1976 CAP allocation. In its 1979 Final Environmental Statement on the CAP's Salt–Gila

Aqueduct, the bureau noted that "Reclamation concurs with the AWC methodology . . ." In its June 1978 Water Conservation report, AWC stated: "The national use rate from public water systems plus rural domestic use, but excluding self-supplied industry, is about 154 gpcd, while in Arizona the comparable average use rate is about 220 gpcd."

A July 8, 1981 Phoenix City Council report placed the current per capita consumption at 240 gpd but added that with lawn irrigation the figure "jumps to about 300 gpd."

Tucson experienced its highest water use in 1974 with 205 gpd, and through their "beat the peak" campaign reduced it to 145 gpd in 1978 and 140 gpd in 1979. The Water Commission's 1975 report lists 55 gpd as the water use in Ajo Heights, in the desert west of Tucson.

Groundwater

The Arizona Water Commission's 1977 Phase II report projects that Maricopa County, which encompasses the Phoenix area, will deplete 331,000 af a year in 1990. The capacity of the reservoirs on the SRP system is 2 million acre feet. The 2020 A.D. urban depletion is projected at 478,000 af. AWC's 1975 Phase I report shows 105,000,000 af of groundwater in storage under the Phoenix area to a depth of 700 feet. An additional 49,600,000 af are in storage to a depth of 1200 feet.

The amount of groundwater stored under central Arizona is 627,000,000 while the total amount in storage under the entire state is 1.19 billion acre feet. The capacity of the 13 largest reservoirs in the nation is 175 million af, and the more than 1500 largest man-made reservoirs is less than 400 maf.

AWC I estimates that there are 216.1 maf of groundwater in storage under Pima County, where Tucson is located, to a depth of 1200 feet. AWC II projects depletions for the county ranging from 269,000 af to 564,000 af for all uses in 2020 A.D.. This means that the county can continue to mine its groundwater for 383 to 800 years.

These vast quantities led to the following statement by L. C. Murphy, Mayor of Tucson, to the U.S. Congress on April 5, 1978:

I do not intend to indulge in the kind of scare tactics sometimes employed when matters of water projects are discussed. Tucson will not dry up and blow away without CAP. What will happen is the heavy reliance on mining groundwater will be continued in the future at ever increasing costs until the resource is depleted.

The mayor then discussed the energy element of groundwater mining, without mentioning that the average depth to the water table in the Tucson area is less than 400 feet while the CAP will pump water uphill more than 2100 feet.

According to the CAP Position Statement of the Southern Arizona Branch of the American Society of Civil Engineers, the amount of the water recharged (renewable) in the Tucson area is "between 50,000 and 130,000 af according to various 'authorities'!" This 1974 analysis accepted 100,000 af. The June 1982 report on the Tucson Active Management Area by the Arizona Department of Water Resources (formerly AWC) uses 75,000 af/year, while AWC II (1977) used 72,000.

AWC II projects urban depletions in 1990 at 72,000 af. This was at a use rate of 190 gpd and a depletion rate of 89 gpd (53% becomes wastewater). At the lower use rate actually experienced by Tucson in the late 1970s (140 gpd), urban depletions would be more than balanced by the dependable supply. Osterkamp shows recharge over 130,000 af.

The June 1982 report shows 1990 municipal depletion at 62,000 af but adds "industrial" depletions of 42,000. Mining consumes 61,000 and Indian agriculture 35,000. Non-Indian agriculture depletes fully 146,000 af. Seventy-five percent of the area's irrigated acreage is in Avra Valley. In a January 8, 1975, letter to the Tucson City Council, Civil Engineer George W. Barr Jr. proposed retiring this acreage at a cost of $7/af — a fraction of the CAP cost.

Tucson began acquiring Avra Valley land in the 1970s. There are 16 maf in storage there. A 1973 report for the city labeled the CAP as the 9th most favorable water supply and noted retirement of irrigated lands as the 7th and 8th most favorable, resulting in an estimated life of groundwater supply at 620 and 1700 years. The county supervisors opposed the CAP in 1973, as the other 6 proposals, ranging from "do nothing" to conservation, showed supplies would last for 100 to 200 years. The City Council vacillated but the County Democratic Committee backed President Carter's withdrawal of funds for the CAP in 1977.

The Tucson area has 28 maf stored under the Upper Santa Cruz Basin to a depth of 700 feet and another 28 maf to 1200 feet. An additional 15 maf is stored under the Altar north and west of Tucson, according to AWC I. Elimination of non-Indian agriculture indicates that the Tucson area would consume less than 300,000 af in 2024 A.D., according to the June 1982 report. AWC II shows depletion of almost 400,000 af in 2020 A.D. since it estimates 4 times more water for mining.

There are 500 million af stored under the counties where Phoenix and Tucson are located and more than 325 maf under the Phoenix, Tucson and Mesa Active Management Areas (AMA). The 1980 groundwater law requires a balance between withdrawal and recharge by 2025 A.D.. The capital cost of the CAP, according to Interior's 1977 review, was $110/af and operation and maintenance costs were $50/af in January 1982, according to the bureau's Project Data Sheet. Thus the value of this unused groundwater is more than $50 billion in today's dollars.

According to AWC's July 1975 report (Table 13), there are 1,192,000,000 acre feet in storage under Arizona and 627,000,000 af of groundwater in central Arizona. The overdraft in these areas is 2,188,000 and 1,789,000 af respectively, according to the same source. Thus the supply could last 545 and 350 years and this is only to depths of 1200 feet.

The Salt River Project

The statement that Phoenix could support New York City's 7 million people on its existing water supply in the Salt and Verde Rivers was made by the executive director of the Arizona Municipal Water Users Association in a documentary by the local CBS affiliate KOOL-TV. According to Smith and Stockton, the annual flow of the Salt River from 1914 to 1979 was 626,800 af. Bulletin 180 of the Arizona Bureau of Mines shows the average flow of the Verde from 1888 to 1966 as 485,800 af. This gives a total of 1.113 million af. At 140 gpd this water would support 7 million people. AWC 1 shows surface diversions from the two rivers as

883,000 af, which indicates a loss of more than 200,00 af from reservoirs, etc. Adding 31,500 af (61,000 in Bull. 180) from the Aqua Fria and 193,000 af (342,100 in Bull. 180) from the Gila River gives enough water for more than 7 million people, even considering the losses.

The case of *Hurley v. Abbott* in the Third Judicial District of the Territory of Arizona, filed March 10, 1910, decided the water rights of the lands within the Phoenix area. Known as the "Kent Decree" because it was decided by Chief Justice Kent sitting as District Judge, it appropriated the first water coming down the Salt and Verde Rivers to lands that had put the water to beneficial use in 1869 "for the economical and successful irrigation and cultivation of such land . . ." These lands are now urbanized.

The Statement of Mayor Margaret Hance of Phoenix, Arizona to the Senate Subcommittee on Public Works Appropriation, dated March 31, 1978, was preceded by the following:

However, in terms of our need, I would like to explain one problem that somehow doesn't seem to get much attention in these general discussions. That involves the many, many Phoenix residents, and metropolitan area residents for that matter, who live outside of the boundaries of the Salt River Project.

SRP permits Phoenix and surrounding cities to deliver its water to their citizens who live "off-project" but this is only a loan. The cities are required to pump water from wells that are off-project and return this water to SRP canals. This wastes energy and causes subsidence.

SRP delivers 35,000 af/yr approximately to the Roosevelt Water Conservation District southeast of the project boundaries. This was contracted for in 1924 when RWCD agreed to line SRP canals. Buckeye Irrigation District receives 1.1% of SRP diversions under a 1942 court settlement (approximately 9000 af/yr). Roosevelt Irrigation District west of Project boundaries is entitled to pump an average of 145,000 af of groundwater a year based upon an agreement entered into at the time the western portion of SRP was waterlogged. This surely indicates that SRP can enter into agreements to allow water to be transferred outside its boundaries.

The subsidy is listed in SRP's *Annual Report* as contributions of power revenues to support water operations. In 1982 it amounted to $13,676,000 while in 1981 it was $4,870,000. Apparently this subsidy is permitted by law (see 1982 Ariz. St. L. J. 497), but it is surely not required.

For a good discussion of SRP, see 1969 Ariz. St. L. J. 636. It began in 1902 as the Salt River Valley Water Users Association and a year later became "the first multi-purpose reclamation project authorized under the Federal Reclamation Act." The major reason for its formation was to contract with the federal government for the repayment of Roosevelt Dam, which was completed in 1911. The federal government transferred operations and maintenance functions to SRP in 1917 but "retained ownership of the Project land and facilities."

In 1937 SRP was granted all the rights and privileges of a municipal corporation, such as exemptions from taxation and the right of eminent domain (Az. Const. art. XIII, §7; ARS §45-902). Thus it is a city and a private association with federal involvements.

In 1982 SRP charged its customers $7.25/af to deliver surface water. Telephone conversations in early 1983 with contractors in the Phoenix area indicated that fill dirt could be delivered at $3.25/cubic yard. An acre foot of dirt amounts to 1500 cubic yards so fill dirt would cost $4875/af.

An acre foot is 43,560 cubic feet, so a ton of water is priced at half a cent. The price of a thousand gallons is 2 cents. Pump water is priced at $25/af. Approximately a third of the water delivered is from wells as SRP pumps substantial amounts into canals and delivers it as less expensive surface water.

SRP and Arizona Public Service are the two large utilities in the Phoenix area. Years ago they divided up the territory and, as a result, SRP water customers can be serviced by APS energy and customers 50 miles outside SRP boundaries receive SRP energy.

SRP has been governed by a 10 member Board of Directors elected in even numbered years on an acreage basis. Primarily due to escalating energy bills, the legislature responded to irate constituents in 1976 and added four directors to be elected at large on a one man-vote basis (ARS 45-961). This, and the rapid urbanization of the area as shown in SRP's *Annual Report*, could solve the problem before the turn of the century.

The 1982 *Arizona State Law Journal* (ASLJ) contains a series of discussions on Special Project Irrigation Districts from page 345 to 527, apparently prompted by the U.S. Supreme Court's decision in *Ball v. James*, 451 U.S. 355 (1981). A good comparison of *Salyer Land Co. v. Tulare Lake Water Storage District*, 410 U.S. 719 (1973) with *Choudry v. Free*, 555 P.2d 438 (1976) is found in 1982 ASLJ.

The quote from the National Water Symposium is from the January 1983 *Engineering Times*, published by the National Society of Professsional Engineers. The symposium was sponsored by that society, the American Society of Civil Engineers, American Public Works Association, American Consulting Engineers Council, and the Water Pollution Control Federation, in cooperation with the National Governor's Association, National League of Cities, U.S. Conference of Mayors, etc.

The Central Arizona Project Association was formed in 1945 to bring Colorado River water to central Arizona. Through 1984 it was still receiving $25,000 a year from the City of Phoenix. Tucson and Pima ceased their $35,000 annual contribution in the mid-1970s. Several of the association's brochures have been titled "Water for People."

The Department of Interior's 1977 review of the CAP came to the following conclusion:

In summary, the cost of water delivered by the Central Arizona Project will be $141 per acre foot. . . . The cost of alternative groundwater sources of supply are currently between $10 and $50 per acre-foot, except in a few places of exceptional groundwater depth . . . Adequate groundwater is generally believed to exist in most places to meet demands over the next 50 years . . .

Agriculture and Economy

The first quote in Chapter 6 is from the "Ending Hunger" briefing held in Phoenix in February 1982. It was sponsored by The Hunger Project, 2015 Steiner St., San Francisco, California. It notes that the current U.N. medium population estimate for the world in A.D. 2000 is 6 billion, but decreasing birth rates have prompted a "recent study" to project 5.5 to 5.8 billion. The rate of growth has slowed from 2% in 1970 to 1.7% per year in 1980.

Professor Paarlberg's comments are from the eighth in a series of 15 articles exploring "Food and People" which appeared March 9, 1982 in the *Phoenix Gazette*.

In March 23, 1983 *Arizona Republic* article notes that U.S. farmers plan to idle 39.4 of the 101.0 million base acres usually planted in corn and sorghum, 32 of 91 million acres in wheat, 6.8 of 15.4 million in cotton, 2.3 of 19 million in barley and oats, and 1.7 of 4 million in rice. Farmers must first sign up for a program that pays them cash to idle 20% of their base acreage, then they can decline to grow crops on an additional 30% to 50% of the base acreage and will be Paid in Kind (PIK) with 80% of the crop they theoretically could grow on that land, according to the *Wall Street Journal* (March 22, 1983).

The Department of Agriculture's 1974 data base indicated that Hawaii consumes the most BTUs per irrigated acre (32 million), closely followed by New Mexico's 26 million and Arizona's 24 million. Next are Nevada and Oklahoma with 12 million each, Kansas and Washington at 10 million each, and Utah and Texas with almost 9 million each. The U.S. average was 7.4 million BTUs per irrigated acre.

The second quote from Howe and Easter continues: ". . . This means that the United States fails to produce its cotton at the lowest cost and in the most efficient manner."

Quotation by William E. Martin, Professor of Agricultural Economics at the University of Arizona is from a May 14, 1974 letter. Professor Martin has twice won the Western Agricultural Economics Association "Outstanding Published Research Award." He noted that the crops which are directly edible, vegetables and citrus, "are seasonal and most are exported to other states." In 1980 these crops accounted for only 7% of Arizona's acreage, which is 5% less than the level Professor Martin was referencing.

In a November 23, 1982, letter, Professor Martin reaffirmed the point, adding that the "price of eggs, poultry and beef is not related to Arizona production of cottonseed. A few acres of vegetables might lower fresh vegetables once in a while." He noted that Arizona feed-lots do not rely on Arizona grain, although they do use some alfalfa. His 1974 letter pointed out that a significant portion of the grains fed to Arizona cattle are imported from Texas and the Midwest.

The figure showing the principal crops harvested in Arizona in 1978 is from the Arizona Crop and Livestock Reporting Service Bulletin S-14, dated April 1979. The Valley Bank's report states that Arizona exports about 90% of its cotton crop, as well as sizable portions of the wheat produced locally.

In 1980 Arizona harvested 631,000 acres of cotton, which consumes 3.5 feet of water per acre. Grains, which consume around 2 feet per acre, accounted for 331,000 acres. This amounts to 2,700,000 af. The statewide overdraft was 2.2 million af (maf), according to AWC I (July 1975).

In 1977, 73% of central Arizona's irrigated acreage was eligible for federal set-asides. In 1980 this had risen to 76%. Upland cotton accounted for 425,000 acres while grain (wheat, barley and sorghum) accounted for 221,000 acres, for a total water consumption of 1.9 maf. CAP promotoers claim it will provide 1.0 to 1.2 maf/year.

Set-aside figures are from a series of articles in March 1982 in the *Arizona Republic* by A. V. Gullette and from phone conversations with the U.S. Department of Agriculture's Stabilization and Conservation Service. Statewide, 778,000 acres are signed up for the program, and 379,000 of those acres would be set aside. In the three central Arizona counties of Maricopa, Pinal and Pima, reductions would occur on 264,000 of the 539,000 acres signed up. One hundred and ninety-nine thousand acres of cotton and 65,000 acres of grains were set aside, for a total water consumption saving of 726,000 af. When combined with hay, which consumes 74 inches/acre/year on the 84,000 acres in central Arizona, the total water consumption would be 1.2 maf. The groundwater overdraft in the area was 1.8 maf according to the Arizona Water Commission's Phase I report.

Since the CAP was authorized in 1968, alfalfa and other hay has accounted for roughly 200,000 acres in Arizona. Since it consumes more than 6 feet per acre per year, hay is the equivalent of the entire CAP supply. The U.S. Depart-

ment of Agriculture shows cotton consuming 41 inches a
season, double-cropped sorghum 54 inches, citrus 4 feet,
while wheat, barley and vegetables consume 2 feet or less
per acre.

The Department of Agriculture Crop and Livestock Reporting Service statistics show that 68% of the cattle shipped
into Arizona in 1979 (the last year reports were issued)
came from Texas, while 63% of Arizona's cattle were exported to California. This pattern was generally typical in
the 1970s. Professor Martin explains that Arizona range
cattle are not accustomed to the desert heat since they graze
in the higher country. They are shipped elsewhere to be
fattened, and Arizona imports Texas cattle which have
adapted to the heat. He adds that that most beef from
feedlots is slaughtered elsewhere because of slaughter plant
efficiencies.

A 1977 report by the California Department of Water
Resources throws more light on this confusing topic. It notes
that historically cattle feeding has been economically favored by low transportation costs and status as an income
tax shelter. In 1972 cattle feeding crops accounted for 69%
of the net water demand in California. The report projected
an 85% reduction in interregional transportation if Texas
cattle were fed in the Midwest. This potential reduction
amounts to 4 billion ton miles in transportation, largely
highway.

On August 4, 1982, a Colorado natural resources
specialist suggested that the West should get out of the
livestock business. Dr. Roger Eldridge, who directs the Colorado Commission on Higher Education, told the Governor's
Commission on Arizona Environment that ranching should
be left to the humid East where water and grass are more
abundant.

Arizona's Personal Income is derived from the following:
table 1-1 of Kelso's 1973 book provides the 1940 to 1970
figures; the 1980 percentages were derived from the Valley
National Bank's 1981 Arizona Statistical Review, Labor
and Proprietors' Income by Industry; dividends, interest,
rent, and transfer payments are not included. Other major
sources of personal income include government 19%, ser-

vices 17%, wholesale and retail trade 17%, construction 9%, transportation and public utilities 7%. Gross State Product from March 1, 1976 Arizona Office of Economic Planning and Development report by H. M. Kaufman, T. L. Beckhelm, and W. M. Hannigan, which showed only 3% from farms in 1975. Employment figures are from the 1970 Census. In July 1984, Tom R. Rex of the ASU Business College reported that agriculture's 3% share of the Gross State Product made it the smallest of Arizona's nine industries.

According to a June 16, 1981 *Arizona Republic* news article (AP), Ben Hill Jr., vice president of Arizona Bank and a member of the national and state economic development councils, made the statement on tourism.

Dr. Kelso, Professor Emeritus of Agricultural Economics at the University of Arizona and formerly Chief of Land Economics at the U.S. Department of Agriculture, shows in Table 7-4 of his book that 0.07 percent will be the net decline in value of all incomes in Arizona as percentage of 1966 total income, due to rising groundwater costs confronting agriculture. His co-author, Professor Martin, notes in his 1981 letter that University of Arizona Agricultural Experiment Station Technical Bulletin 235 is a partial update of their 1973 study and the conclusions do not change.

Among Kelso's conclusions are the followong:

1. Water is *economically* scarce in Arizona but not so *physically* limited as to be a serious threat to the viability of the state's economy.

2. Much of the scarce water supplies are, by legal devices and by reasons of location, locked into uses in which the marginal value of the product of the water is extremely low — approaching zero in some cases.

3. Curtailment of these low-valued uses will have but modest effects on the state's economy.

4. Changing the structure of the state's economy by curtailing water uses producing lowest net incomes can release growth of the Arizona economy from all restraint by water well into the twenty-first century.

The report on Energy and U.S. Agriculture used a 1974 data base, which indicated Arizona crops and livestock were valued at 1.02% of the total U.S. value of $100 billion.

Arizona's $649 million crops were 1.05% of the total value
of the nation's crops. Arizona ranked first in BTU's per
acre with 24.5 milion. This was more than four times the
national average.

Table A-1 shows Arizona's irrigated acreage since the
CAP was authorized in 1968. It is interesting to note that
major funding for the CAP began in 1973. The next years
saw a substantial increase in acreage, with 1.38 million in
1979 and 1.37 in 1981. Most of this increase was in cotton
and grains, with cotton acreage exceeding 600,000 acres in
the period 1979 through 1981.

NUMBER OF ACRES DEVOTED TO ARIZONA'S PRINCIPAL CROPS

Year	Alfalfa	Citus	Cotton	Grains	Vegetables	Total Acres
1968	202,000	49,545	298,000	501,000	91,280	1,204,000
1969	188,000	49,740	310,000	477,000	89,800	1,222,100
1970	205,000	50,050	274,000	496,000	85,900	1,219,030
1971	201,000	50,050	273,800	500,000	81,020	1,205,170
1972	215,000	62,903	285,400	463,000	80,000	1,205,080
1973	219,000	65,280	309,000	485,000	74,700	1,277,600
1974	215,000	68,120	425,000	492,000	73,050	1,352,970
1975	215,000	67,590	298,000	612,000	63,370	1,376,820
1976	210,000	58,510	348,000	684,000	63,600	1,429,210
1977	210,000	56,310	556,500	335,000	65,600	1,327,670
1978	206,000	52,650	572,200	296,000	65,820	1,298,220

Note: Not all crops are shown. Other Crops included in
Total. Source: Arizona Crop & Livestock Reporting Service,
Arizona Agricultural Statistics 1978.

There was an excellent series of articles by Ted Rushton
in the *Mesa Tribune* and the *Tempe Daily News* in December
1980 discussing farm taxation. The Maricopa County Asses-
sor's office generally affirmed their accuracy. Relatively
minor changes have been made in the law since then but
not sufficient to prevent lower taxes by grazing a few sheep.

Conservation and Waste
Space Age technology provides the ultimate conservation
device. The system is initially filled with 1500 gallons of
water which is continually treated to drinking water standards while being recycled. This essentially reduces consumption to 0 gpd.

The PureCycle system had been installed in about 50 homes in Colorado, according to a February 5, 1981, *New York Times* article, and had been approved by Arizona, Wyoming and New Mexico. According to a February 23, 1981, *Newsweek* article, the cost was $15,000. There was also a monthly fee, according to the company's Boulder office. The product has been temporarily discontinued.

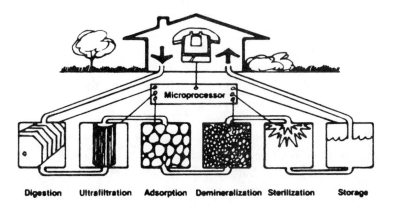

Fig. 53 The Pure Cycle system.

In a March 8, 1972, letter, the Executive Director of AWC noted that the the estimated depletion for median residential areas with piped domestic supply was 1.4 af/ac, and 1.8 with gravity irrigation added. He also noted that vegetables deplete 2.0 af/ac. Thus groundwater mining could end. The April 1978 report by Beard Engineers shows the total dependable supply for the Phoenix area as 931,000 af/yr while total depletion decreases to 921,700 af/yr by 2000 A.D.

A good discussion of "Pricing as a Means of Motivating Better Use" is found in Chapter 7(c) of the National Water Commission's report.

In its 1966 publication, the CAP Association noted that 7,672 miles of the 12,000 miles of farm ditch in Arizona had been lined or piped at a $50 million cost, reducing seepage "losses" by an estimated 387,000 af/yr. These improvements are frequently funded by the federal government, under programs like the Small Reclamation Projects Act.

The former policy of the Arizona Supreme Court is summarized in *City of Glendale v. Sutter*, 54 Ariz. 326, 95 P.2d 569 (1939): . . . farming and mining are so essential to the prosperity and welfare of the state that it was against public policy to make construction and maintenance of open canals, ditches, flumes and 'various means of diversion' for irrigation a ground of negligence." See also "Tort Immunity of Irrigation Districts: An Unattractive Nuisance," 15 Ariz. L. Rev. 172 (1973). According to Professor John Leshy in 1982 Ariz. St. L.J. 345, 358, FN 60, Cal. Gov't. Code 831.8 (West 1980) seems to confer more limited immunity on irrigation districts.

Six vertical feet of water evaporates from the surface of swimming pools, small lakes and canals, on average. Large lakes evaporate more due to wind and wave action, etc. Bartlett, for example, loses 10 feet a year according to weather bureau records, which indicate that the average evaporation from Salt and Verde lakes is greater than 8 feet. If all these reservoirs are full, their surface area is 27,300 acres. AWC I places the average at 70,000 af. It also shows the average evaporation for the state at 198,000 plus 1,149,000 for Lakes Mead, Havasu, and Mohave.

The figures for the fertilizer content of Tucson wastewater was provided by the Cortaro-Marana Irrigation District in the 1981 USDA report, while the energy consumption is from Rawlins. Buckeye I.D. figures are also from USDA report.

The Central Arizona Project

The history of the Bureau of Reclamation is basically from Gates' 1968 history. According to the USDA's publication on *Irrigation with Sewage Effluent* there are 53 shareholders/owners and family farm units of 250 acres average size within the boundaries of the Cortaro-Marana Irrigation District.

Young's paper was delivered at the forum on "The Arizona Water Controversy," sponsored by the Arizona Academy of Science, Flagstaff, May 11, 1968, before he left his position as Associate Professor of Agricultural Economics at the University of Arizona. In a 1967 paper, Kelso quotes the 1960 textbook on water supply by Hirshleifer, et. al.:

> ... the "water is different" ... philosophy ... might be only amusing if it did not lead to some political actions having very serious implications; in particular, it has led to the near-universal view that private ownership is unseemly or dangerous for a type of property so uniquely the common concern of all.

The bureau's January 1, 1983, Project Data Sheet for the CAP shows the total cost as $2,894,367,000. Note 18 indicates another $107 million should be added for the distribution system. The Schedule of Construction program uses $408 million for the Regulatory Storage Division, which is the old Orme Dam plan, as discussed later. The Bureau's selected alternative would cost between $978 million and $1.16 billion. Therefore total CAP costs in 1983 dollars would be $3.57 to $3.75 billion.

Reclamation farmers are allowed an initial development period of 10 years during which no capital charges are payable; thereafter, they are given 40 years to repay the capital at no interest charge. While this is the largest component of the subsidy, according to the National Water Commission's 1973 report, electric power revenues, municipal and industrial water sales and "allocation, to an unwarranted extent, of joint costs of multipurpose projects to nonirrigation features" are additional sources.

Dr. Power's report cites numerous reports from Arizona, Utah, and Colorado placing the value of an additional acre foot of water around $15. Kelso's study indicated $15.96 (in 1977 dollars), the U.S. Forest Service's Chaparral Conversion Project in Arizona used $15.57, the Salt River Project estimated $15.79. Howe and Young in Utah came up with $15/af while Young found Colorado's average to be $14.50. This is for the last units of water used. Classic economic theory holds that this would be the value of any new water provided. Generally it would be used to grow alfalfa, the least valuable crop. Otherwise the prudent farmer would grow a higher value crop on his existing alfalfa fields if the demand were there.

The following table from Dr. Power's 1978 CAP report shows the immensity of the federal subsidy:

Type of Federal Subsidy	Total cumulative subsidy	Value of subsidy in 1977 dollars
Irrigation— interest (7% - 0%)	$3,056,410,000	$ 602,728,000
Irrigation interest during construction*	315,000,000	315,000,000
M&I—interest (7% - 3.342%)	461,610,000	215,280,000
Non-irrigation interest during construction*	140,072,000	140,072,000
Non-reimbursable cost (Indian water, flood control, etc.)	1,498,000,000	427,647,000
Federal Subsidy	$5,471,092,000	$1,700,727,000

Compounded forward to first year of operation which is year of present values — explaining why the entries are identical in both columns.

The 1973 Hannon-Bezdek study showed that 7% more jobs would be created with mass transit construction, 30% more by shifting water projects money to Social Security benefits, and 57% more via National Health Insurance.

Interior's 1977 CAP review presents an Alternative Economic Analysis which states:

. . . Given these existing costs of water to municipal and industrial users, the benefits of $200 per acre foot for municipal and industrial water that were calculated in the benefit-cost analysis for the Central Arizona Project are questionable. If the Central Arizona Project were not built, it is uncertain that an alternative single purpose aqueduct would be built by municipal and industrial users acting on their own.

. . . Thus, although the net revenues from powerplant operation prior to commencement of the Central Arizona Project can be counted as benefits of the project in an accounting sense, they are not benefits in the sense that their realization depends on whether or not the project is built.

. . . because the terms for the Navajo Powerplant were set some time ago, the costs of electric power obtained by the Central Arizona Project will be significantly less than it would cost to go into the market now to buy power for 1985. . . . Since the Central

Arizona Project's use of power will force others to develop new power sources of equivalent magnitude for their own needs in 1985, the true cost to society of the project's power use is the cost of new power sources that have to be developed. (Put another way, if the Central Arizona Project were not built, its power supplies in later years could be sold for going market prices that would be much higher than the allowance for power costs in the benefit-cost analysis.)

. . . the value calculated for irrigation water . . . is based on the assumption that relatively small decreases in water availability impose economic losses in agricultural production that (per acre-foot) are just as large as would result from the total loss of water availability. This procedure does not take account of the fact that, up to some point, farmers can conserve to reduce water use with smaller economic losses compared with the losses that (per acre-foot) would be caused by a *total* loss of water availability.

These benefit-cost ratios may still be over-estimated in some respects . . .

The Last Waterhole

The U.S.G.S. study shows losses from Lakes Mead and Mohave and the Colorado River from the Lee's Ferry Compact point to Davis Dam at .982 maf and gains at less than 0.5 maf in 1990 when they predicted Upper Basin Depletion would be 5.1 maf. The study noted that losses associated with storage and conveyance of water below Davis dam are about 0.9 maf. It adds that the usable part of the small inflow below Davis Dam probably is little greater than the excess flow to Mexico that will be necessary to effect delivery of the guaranteed quantity as requested by Mexico.

The Bureau's 1975 *Westwide Study* shows Upper Basin demand could reach 5.8 maf as early as 1993. Their prediction of a shortage in the entire basin by 1992 comes from the 1979 GAO study:

. . . assuming an average annual virgin flow of about 14.8 maf, the Bureau has conducted several studies . . . Some of the earlier studies showed that sufficient water would be in the river system to meet basin water demands until sometime after 1985 when the Central Arizona Project (CAP) is scheduled to make initial deliveries. After this period, the river will probably not yield enough water under normal circumstances to meet all basin demands, the Mexican treaty obligations, and river system losses. More recent Bureau studies indicate that a shortage of water could occur as early as 1992 and probably would occur prior to 2023 . . .

Since the Power report the Indian allotment has been increased, especially for the years following 2005. Again this analysis is based upon 14.8 maf being available, since that is the number used by the Arizona Department of Water Resources. Much of this belief depends on records prior to 1921 before the river was accurately gauged.

Back in 1944, Mr. G. E. P. Smith, a civil engineer who was then a professor of Agricultural Engineering at the University of Arizona, wrote the Arizona State Land Commissioner and explained how the early estimates were obtained:

1) The river flow — that is, the discharge of the river — was not really measured at or near Lee's Ferry until June, 1921. The records of flow from 1895 up to that time were estimated by various comparisons to a certain extent, but mostly by guess-work, from measurements that had been taken at Yuma and some few stations on tributaries, and from rainfall data, which as you know is extremely variable from place to place, so that a few stations do not truly represent the whole area.

2) The station at Yuma where measurements began in 1902 was below the mouth of the Gila, and since the output of the Gila was being measured separately, it added an uncertain factor which could not be eliminated when trying to utilize the Yuma records to build up a hypothetical record at Lee's Ferry.

3) The Yuma station did not have good control . . .

4) Stream gauging equipment 40 years ago was very crude as compared to the equipment used today. I think it was in the early 20's when great advances were made in the design and construction of the equipment . . .
It gives me no pleasure to submit this criticism . . .

It seems strange that the bureau would base its planning on such uncertain records while rejecting the sophisticated dendrochronological analysis of Dr. Stockton.

The other two Colorado Projects that were authorized with the CAP were San Miguel in southwestern Colorado and West Divide in west central Colorado.

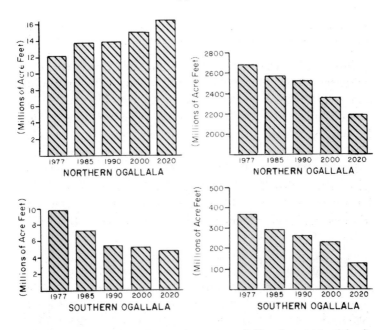

NORTHERN OGALLALA

NORTHERN OGALLALA

SOUTHERN OGALLALA

SOUTHERN OGALLALA

Fig. 54 Ogallala Aquifer: Annual water use rates (left) and water remaining in storage (right). *U.S. Department of Commerce.*

NAWAPA was the subject of an article in the May 15, 1977, issue of *Forbes*. A March 25, 1976, letter to the author from Roland Kelley, Vice President, Environmental and Water Engineering for the Ralph M. Parsons Company continued: ". . . and the proposed utilization of the NAWAPA waters in the area was conceived on the assumption that the Central Arizona Project would be built and placed in operation." Lyndon H. LaRouche, Jr., former Presidential candidate and Chairman of the National Democratic Policy Committee's advisory board, wrote a lengthy article on NAWAPA in the January 19, 1982, *Executive Intelligence Review*.

The material on the Ogallala Aquifer is from the 1982 "Six-State High Plains-Ogallala Aquifer Area Regional Study," a chapter by H.O. Banks in *Western Water Resources*, by the Federal Reserve Bank of Kansas City, and on Gooch's water importation paper which was presented at the Texas Section, American Society of Civil Engineers' convention March 26, 1982.

Publication 1689 by the National Academy of Sciences states: "Early Bureau of Reclamation studies indicated that a total of 580,000 acres in the Yuma area could be irrigated from the Colorado River . . . At present, 71,200 acres have been developed." Gruen Association, Inc. of Los Angeles was commissioned by the Maricopa Association of Governments in August 1975 to study future growth in central Arizona.

As of 1980, Arizona had almost 200,000 acres to select from federal holdings. These are the remaining entitlements to lands granted Arizona upon statehood, commonly known as state lands or school trust lands (because income from them is to be used to help pay for schools).

The productivity of lands in western Arizona is similar to that in central Arizona, with a higher productivity per acre for upland cotton, the state's most abundant crop, according to U.S. reports.

The $100/af differential is based upon the EDF study. Pumping Colorado River water to the LA area in 1986 dollars would cost $412/af plus a marginal salinity cost of $162/af for a total of $574/af. State Water Project (SWP) supplies average 300 mg/1 while Colorado River Aqueduct water averaged 706 mg/1 (tds) in 1980-81).

The marginal cost for a twenty year supply of the first 48,150 af (through wastewater reclamation) would cost $609/af. EDF's plan to conserve water in Imperial I.D. and transfer it to southern California would cost $682/af for 350,000 af. Additional "new" water would cost $709 to $1,163/af. The Peripheral Canal supply would cost $718/af for 700,000 af.

According to the Seven Party Agreement of 1931, the first 3.85 maf of Colorado River water goes to three irrigation districts, primarily Imperial I.D. The next 0.55 maf goes to MWD for the 4.4 maf total. The next 0.55 also goes to MWD, then 0.112 to San Diego, and 0.3 to irrigation districts for a total allocation of 5.362 maf. However only 4.8 maf was utilized in 1980 and EDF projects a shortage of 0.4 maf. A "new" supply of this amount would cost around $100/af ($682 vs. $574/af) or $40 million. If SWP contracts are to be enforced, the state could use the full amount that could be supplied by the Colorado River Aqueduct (1.2 maf/yr). The additional 800,000 af would be more expensive and the cost could be more than $80 million a year.

A 1977 Bureau publication (GPO 1977-240-951/12) on Glenn Canyon Dam notes that it generates a million kilowatts or "enough to meet the electric energy needs of a city with a population of 1.5 million." CAP needs 547,000 kilowatts and SWP lift is even greater, although it would be noted that SWP does generate some energy as the lifted water flows downhill again.

Actually AWC II projects steam electric depletions as high as 534,000 af for Maricopa County in 2020 for Alternative future I. Alternatives II and III use 279,000 af. Arizona Revised Statute 30-125 gives first preference when power supplies are insufficient to Districts, which are defined as Power, or Water Districts under ARS title 45 which includes the Salt River Project. Second preference is for "Any incorporated city or town . . ." Mesa, a suburb of Phoenix, does have access to Colorado River energy.

The AAES Coordinating Committee on Energy statement II was reported in the May 1983 issue of ASCE news. Its chairman noted that U.S. energy demand may increase more than 30% by 2000.

AWC II shows the overdraft at 2.2 maf and total water use at 4.8. Thus 46% is mined. Assuming 46% of Arizona's irrigated land is retired at $1000/acre for roughly 550,000 acre amounts to $550 million.

ARS 45-611 provided for an annual $2 per acre foot fee for "purchasing and retiring grandfathered rights." ARS 45-566 permits this to begin no earlier than 2006. Even if this occurred in 1979 at $1000/acre, the cost would be approximately $550 million. With 2.5 maf of groundwater being pumped, the revenue would amount to $5 million a year. By 2006 land values will be considerably higher and presumably the amount of water pumped will be much lower.

The salinity of the Colorado River is somewhat variable, depending on flow, etc. The average total dissolved solids (tds) below Parker between 1974 and 1978 was 696 ppm and in 1981 it was 723 ppm. The EPA has approved standards adopted by the Colorado River Basin Salinity Control Forum which would result in an annual flow-weighted average tds of 747 mg/1, which is essentially equal to 750 ppm.

Orme and Other Dams

Much of the background information for the chapters on this subject is contained in notes, memoranda, reports, etc., from the author's involvement in the decade long Orme controversy, in addition to the larger reports cited in the bibliography. The flood history of the Salt River as presented to the Governor's Advisory Committee by the LA District Corps of Engineers on August 28, 1980 follows:

Flood History

    a.   Pre SRP Construction Floods
        1891 (Feb) — 300,000 CFS
        1905 (Apr) — 115,000 CFS
        1905 (Nov) — 200,000 CFS
    b.   SRP Construction Period Floods
        Salt River Construction — 1908 through 1930 —
        (1911 — Roosevelt)
        Verde River Construction — 1939 Horseshoe (50
          mod), 1945 Bartlett

1916 (Jan) —	120,000
1920 (Feb) —	130,000
1938 (Mar) —	95,000
1941 (Mar) —	40,000

    c.   1941-1965 No Significant Flows
    d.   Post SRP Construction Floods

1965 (Dec) —	70,000
1973 (Feb — May)	20,000
1978 (Mar) —	120,000
1978 (Dec) —	140,000
1979 (Jan) —	100,000
1979 (Mar) —	70,000
1980 (Feb) —	180,000

The history of the dam safety controversy on the Salt River is interesting. On June 2, 1970, the Bureau's Chief

Engineer in Denver forwarded to their Boulder City, Nevada, Regional Director reconnaissance level designs and cost estimates for raising Roosevelt dam and modifying Stewart Mountain dams for safety purposes. In 1977 the bureau told Congress that in the case of Roosevelt: "If the maximum probable flood were to occur, the water in the reservoir would rise approximately 2.5 feet above the top of the dam parapet and the dam would fail." The same report said Stewart Mountain dam would not fail.

According to the February 14, 1979 *Arizona Republic* story on CCAP's testimony, the head of the Bureau in Arizona stated that his studies have shown that Roosevelt and Steward Mountain Dams are safe. SRP continued to maintain that their dams were not unsafe, called the conditions contemplated "highly improbable" but did not point out that the Bureau's 1977 analysis stated: "Under present operating restrictions the normal water level in the (Roosevelt) reservoir has been reduced to protect against failure during intermediate floods." SRP said they should be able to avoid failure during the MPF by anticipating when flooding might occur and releasing water to make room for runoff. Yet one year later a flow that was only 75% of the old MPF caused SRP to advise the Governor to prepare for the failure of Stewart Mountain Dam.

CCAP also presented testimony to Congress in the spring of 1979, asking that Roosevelt be repaired as soon as possible. In a July 5, 1979, letter, the bureau's D.C. office stated that the integrity of Roosevelt's structure would not be in danger during an MPF but "With sustained outflow of 150,000 ft cfs there would be overtopping and the damage to the spillway chute could result in water eroding the foundation of the left thrust block which could cause failure of the dam."

The May 1981 bureau report showed three acceptable options for Bartlett with a 27 foot raise and gated spillway at $85 million being the lowest cost. Two were approved for Horse shoe with $125 for a gated spillway the lowest cost. Allowing failure of Horseshoe and replacing the dam afterwards for $185 million was combined with a $110 million option for Bartlett that was not listed as acceptable, and that combination was listed "At this time, option not acceptable." In this report Cliff was estimated to cost $193 and the bureau notes that it appears to be the least cost method, yet five months later Cliff's cost was listed as $241 million in the CAWCS study.

The bureau did consider building an auxiliary spillway that would permit the MPF to be routed safely around the dams. This solution was rejected because they are ". . . rarely used by the Bureau of Reclamation and then only when the section is short in length and height. Sections of this magnitude as estimated for Horseshoe and Bartlett Dams are not used . . ." Yet in September 1980, the consulting engineer firm of Camp, Dresser and McKee made a presentation to a CAWCS meeting which included a Horseshoe spillway 4,500 feet wide at a cost of $53,800,000 and a Bartlett spillway with a 1,200 foot wide channel for only $8 million. It also showed that a new Horseshoe would cost $150 to $184 million.

In April 1981 CDM completed its Stage II report under a contract with the Corps of Engineers, showing total construction costs for the Horseshoe spillway about $54 million and $8 million for Bartlett. They noted the emergency auxiliary spillways ". . . were designed to safely pass the PMF while allowing the existing structures to remain undamaged. A type "A "auxiliary spillway as shown in the EM 1110-2-1603 was used at both dam sites."

The referenced Engineering Manual was issued by the Corps of Engineers on March 31, 1965. At section 45, it defines a "fuseplug spillway" as an embankment intended to wash out during an extreme flood. It adds:

. . . a more conservative plan would be a low section for initial breaching by erosion, but with provisions for blasting a breach in case of an emergency when it is desirable to lower the reservoir level more rapidly.

Actual experience with the operation of a fuseplug spillway appears lacking. The Corps of Engineers has used fuseplug levees or planned crevasses on the Mississippi River levee system. The breaching operations of the Birds Point-New Madrid Floodway levees below Cairo and at Caernarvon below New Orleans are examples. The Aluminum Company of America has built fusesplug spillways in connection with dams in the southern Appalachians, but there is no operating experience with these spillways.

Small wonder that there is no operating experience. Maximum probable floods occur less than half as frequently as 3,000 year events. In fact, they are so infrequent that the bureau does not put a frequency on them, then uses that as the reason they cannot do a risk analysis, which was recommended by the Central Chapter of the Arizona Chapter of Professional Engineers in 1982.

Public Law 93-251 (88 Stat. 32), March 7, 1974, section 73(a) begins: "In the survey, planning, or design by any Federal agency of any project involving flood protection, consideration shall be given to . . ." The government, after years of foot dragging, was finally looking into practical non-structural alternatives when the MPF was tripled and Cliff Dam became the only solution in their mind.

Subsidence

Much of the soil under Arizona's desert valleys consists of sand and gravel. Water is stored in the voids between these particles. According to the 1975 study of groundwater by California's Department of Water Resources, subsidence (the lowering of the surface of the land) occurs when groundwater is squeezed from the clay lenses that are sometimes interspersed within the sand and gravel underground basin. The clay consolidates, occupying a smaller volume.

According to Tucson's 1973 CAP report, in San Jose, California, subsidence of 35 feet was measured, but no significant damage to surface facilities occurred. The same is true at Long Beach, California with a settlement of more than 20 feet. Other areas have experienced similar types of subsidence. In his 1981 paper, Poland provides a good discussion of subsidence:

Subsidence due to ground-water withdrawal develops principally under two contrasting environments. and mechanics. One environment is that of carbonate rocks overlain by unconsolidated deposits, or old sinkholes filled with unconsolidated deposits, that receive buoyant support from the ground-water body. When the water table is lowered, buoyant support is lost and the hydraulic gradient increased, the unconsolidated material may move downward into openings in the underlying carbonate rocks, sometimes causing catastrophic collapses of the roof. In Alabama, an estimated 4,000 man-induced sinkholes have formed since 1900 in contrast to less than 50 natural collapses (16). In the United

States the occurrence of manmade sinkholes is common in carbonate terrane from Florida to Pennsylvania, numbering many thousands. The individual sinkhole area is small, however, usually within the range of 10,000 m^2.

The other and by far the most extensive occurrence is that of young unconsolidated or semiconsolidated sediments of high porosity laid down in alluvial, lacustrine, or shallow marine environments. All areas are underlain by semiconfined or confined aquifer systems containing aquifers of sand or gravel, or both, of high permeability and low compressibility interbedded with clayey aquitards of low vertical permeability and high compressibility under virgin stresses. Most of the compacting deposits were normally loaded, or approximately so, before man applied stresses exceeding preconsolidation stress (maximum past stress). These aquifer systems compact in response to increased effective stress caused by artesian-head decline in the coarse-grained aquifers and time-dependent pore-pressure reduction in the fine-grained compressible aquitards, causing land-surface subsidence. Note that from Savannah, Ga., to Houston, Texas, the ground-water withdrawal and subsidence are occurring in coastal-plain and shallow marine deposits, whereas from Arizona to northern California, the withdrawal and subsidence are occurring in valley fill, chiefly alluvial-fan and flood-plain deposits.

In Arizona, subsidence is not particularly significant, but differential settlement of the land surface is another matter. This generally occurs when the valley subsides while the mountains, of course, remain stable. Then earth fissures sometimes develop at the interface of the valley and the mountain. The Arizona Water Commission used these cracks to create fears of disaster. The 1973 report by the City of Tucson criticized these "scare tactics" as a "gross misuse of facts."

These fissures are actually nearly vertical cracks, one-half to three-quarters of an inch in width. They are not faults like those associated with earthquakes. Erosion from irrigation water or rainfall widens the fissures to gulleys 2 to 20 feet wide and deep. This creates only "one more problem" for highway engineers. Normal maintenance procedures consist of crack filling, as necessary.

While subsidence damage in urban areas has been minimal, Tucson is continuously phasing out pumping within the central metropolitan area to alleviate this potential threat. Other cities would be well advised to heed the advice in the previously referred to Tucson report:

... the occurrence of subsidence is not necessarily a cause for panic. If it is known in advance that subsidence may occur, many of its potential ill effects can be alleviated or eliminated ...

Potential problems in the Phoenix area can be avoided by using surface water in areas outside SRP boundaries.

Subsidence damage has occurred in agricultural areas, where most of the groundwater mining occurs. A University of Arizona study shows, however, that the damage amounts to only a penny per acre per year. This hardly provides an incentive to reduce pumping.

Bibliography

American Society of Civil Engineers. *The Evaluation of Dam Safety.* Proceedings of Engineering Foundation Conference. December 1976.

American Society of Civil Engineers, Arizona Section, Southern Arizona Section. Position Statement, "CAP and the Tucson Area Water." circa 1974.

Andrus, Cecil D. Memorandum to the President from the Secretary of the Interior. February 14, 1977.

Angelides, S., and E. Bardach. *Water Banking: How to Stop Wasting Agricultural Water.* Institute for Contemporary Studies, San Francisco. 1978.

Arizona Bureau of Mines. U.S. Geological Survey and U.S. Bureau of Reclamation. *Mineral and Water Resources of Arizona.* Bulletin 180, University of Arizona. 1969.

Arizona Department of Economics Planning and Development. *Arizona's Water Allocation Study: An Economic Planning Review.* June 1971.

Arizona Department of Economic Security. *Population Projections, Arizona and Counties.* January 1982.

Arizona Department of Revenue. *Sales Ratio*: Statistical Summary for 1979. July 1979.

Arizona Department of Water Resources, Tucson Active Management Area. *A Water Issues Primer for the Tucson Active Management Area.* June 1982.

Arizona Office of Economic Planning and Development. *Arizona Community Profiles.* Office of the Governor, 1976.

Arizona Revised Statutes 30-125. *Preferences When Power Supplies are Insufficient.* 1947.

Arizona Revised Statutes 45-101 et seq. *Public Nature and Use of Water,* as interpreted by court decisions, eg: Howard v. Perrin (1906) 26 S.Ct. 195, 200 U.S. 71; Bristor v. Cheatham (1953) 75 Ariz. 227, 255 P.2d 173; Neal v. Hunt (1975) 172 Ariz. 307, 541 P.2d 559.

Arizona Revised Statutes 45-401 et seq. *The Arizona Groundwater Management Act.* Senate Bill 1001, 34th Legislature, 4th Special Session, 1980.

Arizona Revised Statutes. Article 4, *Floodplain Management,* Section 45-2341 et seq., effective August 8, 1973.

Arizona Water Commission. *Alternative Futures, Phase II Arizona State Water Plan.* February 1977.

—————. *Inventory of Resource and Uses, Phase 1, Arizona State Water Plan.* July 1975.

—————. *Staff Recommendations Re Allocation of Arizona's Remaining Entitlement in the Colorado River & Specific Recommendations Concerning Allocation of M&I Water Supplies.* November 24, 1976.

—————. *Water Conservation, Phase III — Part 1, Arizona State Water Plan.* June 1978.

Arizona Water Resources Association. "Hydrology and Water Resources in Arizona and the Southwest." Volume 1, Proceedings of the Arizona Section, AWRA, and the Hydrology Section of the Arizona Academy of Science, April 22-23, 1971, Tempe, Arizona.

Atkinson, Rick. "The Next American Crisis," *The Kansas City Times.* May 1981.

Baden, John, ed. *The Vanishing Farmland Crisis: Critical Views of the Movement to Preserve Agricultural Land.* Published for the Political Economy Research Center, Bozeman, Montana. University Press of Kansas, 1984.

Bagley, J.M., K.R. Kimball, and L. Kapaloski. *Feasibility Study of Establishing a Water Rights Banking/Brokering Service in Utah.* UWRL/P-80/02, University of Utah. June 1980.

Ballard, S.C., M.D. Devine, et al. *Water and Western Energy: Impacts, Issues, and Choices.* C.W. Howe, General Editor. Westview Press, 1982.

Beard, Arthur. *Future Environmental Setting, Phoenix Metropolitan Area, EIS - MPFP, Phase 1, Memorandum No. 2.* By Arthur Beard Engineers, Inc. & Camp Dresser & McKee, Inc., April 15, 1978.

—————. *Water Supply and Demand in Maricopa County, Arizona, A Report to the Maricopa Association of Governments.* Prepared by Arthur Beard Engineers, Inc., Phoenix, Arizona, in association with CDM, Inc., Environmental Engineers, Pasadena, California, March 1977.

Behavior Research Center. *Rocky Mountain Poll.* November 1981.

Benson, Lenni Beth. "Desert Survival: The Evolving Western Irrigation District." 1982 Arizona State Law Journal, 377-419.

Berk, R.A., C.J. LaCivita, K. Sredl, and T.F. Cooley. *Water Shortage: Lessons in Conservation from the Great California Drought, 1976-77.* Abt Books, 1981.

Black and Veatch. *Consulting Engineers Report, Offering Statement for Tucson's Water System Revenue Bonds.* Kansas City. May 1977.

The Boulder Canyon Project Act, 45 Stat. 1057 (1928).

Brunton, R.L. *City of Phoenix Water Issues, City Council Report from Development Services Manager to City Manager*. July 8, 1981.

California Department of Water Resources. *California's Ground Water*. Bulletin No. 118, September 1975.

California Department of Water Resources. *Delta Water Facilities*. Bulletin 76, July 1978.

Camp, Dresser & McKee. *Modification to Horseshoe and Bartlett Dams, Stage II — Structural Design and Cost Memo*. Prepared for U.S. Army Corps of Engineers, April 1981.

John Carollo, Engineers. *Water Report, City of Scottsdale, Arizona*. 1975.

Carr, Lynch Associates, Inc. *Rio Salado Development Alternatives*. Prepared for Rio Salado Development District, January 24, 1983.

Central Arizona Project Association. "Saving Water in Arizona." January 1966.

_____. "Water for People." no date.

Citizens for a Responsible CUP. Issues Paper, The Central Utah Project, Part 1. circa 1978.

The Colorado River Basin Project Act, 82 Stat. 885 (1968), Public Law 90-537.

Congressional Budget Office. *Public Works Infrastructure: Policy Considerations for the 1980s*. April 1983.

Cousteau, Jacques-Yves. *The Cousteau Almanac*. The Cousteau Society, 1981.

Dennis, Harry. *Water and Power; the Peripheral Canal and Its Alternatives*. Friends of the Earth Books, 1981.

Dexter, J.R., G.E. Willeke, and L.D. James. "Social Aspects of Flood Proofing." Presented at ASCE conference in Blacksburg, Virginia, July 26-28, 1978.

DeYoung, Tim. "Governing Special Districts: The Conflict Between Voting Rights and Property Privileges," 1982 *Arizona State Law Journal* 419-453.

Duffield, John W. *Auburn Dam: A Case Study*. University of Montana, 1979.

_____. *An Economic Critique of the U.S. Corps of Engineers Red River Waterway Project*. University of Montana, March 1978.

Eastern Pima County Water Resources Coordination Committee. *Report on Central Arizona Project Water Needs*. April 14, 1980.

El-Ashry, M.T. "Alternatives to Current Water Resources Planning in the West, EDF (Denver); Presented at American Water Resources Association meeting in Tucson, Arizona, November 1, 1977.

Environmental Defense Fund. *Trading Conservation Investments for Water*. March 1983.

Erie, L.J., O.F. French, D.A. Bucks, and K. Harris. *Consumptive*

Use of Water by Major Crops in the Southwestern United States. U.S. Department of Agriculture, May 1982.

Fair, Gordon M., and John C. Geyer. *Elements of Water Supply and Waste-Water Disposal.* John Wiley & Sons, Inc., 1971.

Federal Reserve Bank of Kansas City. *Western Water Resources; Coming Problems and the Policy Alternatives.* A Symposium held September 27-28, 1979. Westview Press, 1980.

Forbes. "The World's Biggest Ditch." May 15, 1977.

Gardner, Bruce L. *The Governing of Agriculture.* Published for the International Center for Economic Policy Studies and the Institute for the Study of Market Agriculture by The Regents Press of Kansas, 1981.

Gates, Paul W. *History of Public Land Law Development.* Written for the Public Land Law Review Commission, U.S. Government Printing Office, Washington, D.C. Nov. 1968.

Gehm, H.W., and J.I. Bregman. *Handbook of Water Resources and Pollution Control.* Van Nostrand Reinhold Co. 1976.

Gooch, Thomas C., P.E. "History of Water Importation Plans for Texas." Presented at the Texas Section, ASCE, Spring Convention in Fort Worth, Texas, 1982.

Hannon, B., and R. Bezdek. "Job Impact of Alternatives to Corps of Engineers Projects, Engineering Issues." *Journal of Professional Activities,* American Society of Civil Engineers, vol. 99, October 1973, pp. 521-531.

Hawken, Paul. *The Next Economy.* Holt, Rinehart & Winston, 1981.

Hely, Allen G. *Lower Colorado River Water Supply — Its Magnitude and Distribution.* U.S. Geological Survey Professional Paper 486-D.

Hole, Stanley W., and Peter B. Rhoads. "Water Resources and Growth Management in Florida." *Journal of the Water Resources and Management Division,* American Society of Civil Engineers, October 1982.

Hollon, W. Eugene. *The Great American Desert; Then and Now.* University of Nebraska Press, 1975.

Howe, C.W., and K.W. Easter. *Interbasin Transfers of Water.* John Hopkins University Press, 1971.

Howells, David H., and James C. Warman. "Groundwater Management in the Southeast." *Journal of the Water Resources Planning and Management Division,* American Society of Civil Engineers, October 1982.

Imperial Irrigation District. "The Colorado River and Imperial Valley Soils." 1970.

Interagency Task Force on Orme Dam Alternatives, Flood Control Subcommittee. Flood Control Summary Report, September 1977.

————. Final Report, May 1978.

Johnson, Ralph W. *Major Interbasin Transfers; Legal Aspects.* Legal Study Number 7, National Water Commission, July 26, 1971.

Johnson, James W. *Summary of the 1980 Arizona Groundwater Management Act.* December 1980.

Kahn, Herman, and Paul Bracken. *Arizona Tomorrow.* Hudson Institute, 1979.

Kahrl, W.L. *Water and Power.* University of California Press, 1982.

Keith, J.E., K. Wilde, J.C. Anderson, and A. LeBaron. "Western Economic Development and Water Planning: Bureau of Reclamation." *Journal of the Water Resources Planning and Management Division, American Society of Civil Engineers,* March 1979.

Kelso, Maurice M., William E. Martin, and Lawrence E. Mack. *Water Supplies and Economic Growth in an Arid Environment, An Arizona Case Study.* The University of Arizona Press, 1973.

Kennedy, Burt. *Water.* KOOL-TV (CBS-Channel 10) Documentary, 1978.

Khera, Sigrid, ed., *The Yavapai of Fort McDowell, An Outline of Their History and Culture.* 701 HUD Grant. January 1978.

Kneese, Allen V., and F. Lee Brown. *The Southwest Under Stress.* The Johns Hopkins University Press, 1981.

Kovalic, Joan M. "Funding to Meet America's Water Needs." *Professional Engineer,* Winter 1982.

Lawson, Michael. *Damned Indians: The Pick-Sloan Plan and the Missouri River Sioux.* University of Oklahoma Press, 1982.

Leone, B., and J. Smith. *The Energy Crisis: Opposing Viewpoints.* Greenhaven Press, 1981.

Leshy, John D. "Irrigation Districts in a Changing West — an Overview." 1982 *Arizona State Law Journal* 345-376.

Magnuson, Ed. "The Repairing of America." *Time,* January 10, 1983.

Mann, Dean. *The Politics of Water in Arizona.* The University of Arizona Press, 1963.

Martin, William E. "Economic Magnitudes and Economic Alternatives in Lower Basin Use of Colorado River Water." Presented at Oaxtepec, Mexico, March 15, 1974.

_____, H. M. Ingram, A. H. Griffin, and N. K. Laney, *Saving Water in a Desert City.* Resources for the Future, 1984.

Marum and Marum, Inc. *A Regional Plan for Water, Sewage and Solid Waste Management.* Prepared for Pima Association of Governments by Engineering-Science, Inc., 1973.

McCauley, Charles. "Economic Aspects of Land Subsidence Near Eloy, Arizona." Doctoral Thesis, Department of Hydrology and Water Resources, University of Arizona, circa 1975.

McDowell, John M., and Keith R. Ugone. "The Effect of Institutional Setting on Behavior in Public Enterprises: Irrigation Districts in Western States." 1982 *Arizona State Law Journal* 453-497.

Meyers, C.J., and A.D. Tarlock. *Water Resource Management, A Coursebook in Law and Public Policy.* The Foundation Press, 1971.

Murphy, L.C., Mayor, City of Tucson, Arizona. Statement before U.S. Senate Subcommittee on Public Works Appropriations, April 5, 1978.

National Academy of Sciences. *Final Report, Committee on Nuclear and Alternative Energy Systems.* 1979.

———. *Water and Choice in the Colorado Basin: an Example of Alternatives in Water Management.* Publication 1689, 1968.

———. *Climate, Climactic Change and Water Supply.* National Research Council, 1977.

National Society of Professional Engineers. Position on Water Policy. Adopted, January 1981; Revised, January 1983.

The National Water Commission. *Water Policies for the Future: Final Report to the President and to the Congress.* June 1973.

Officer, James E.F. *Arid-Lands Agriculture and the Indians of the American Southwest.* University of Arizona Press, 1971.

Orange County Water District. *Water Quality and Consumer Costs,* Santa Ana, California, May 1972.

Osterkamp, W.R. *Groundwater Recharge in the Tucson Area.* U.S. Geological Survey Map I-844-E, 1973.

Osterkamp, W.R., and P.P. Ross. *Recoverable Groundwater in the Phoenix Area.* U.S. Geological Survey, Map I-845-K, 1975.

National Water Symposium; Proceedings of the Changing Directions in Water Management — An Infrastructure Financing Policy Symposium. National Society of Professional Engineers, et al, Washington, D.C., Nov. 17-19, 1982.

New Jersey Department of Environmental Protection. *The New Jersey Statewide Water Supply Master Plan.* April 1982.

Nickerson, Steve. *Indian Water Rights.* Institute for the Development of Indian Law, Washington, D.C., 1979.

Pacific Southwest Interagency Committee. *Lower Colorado Region Comprehensive Framework Study.* June 1971.

Pierce, Gaylord. Cartoons on Arizona's Water, Southwest Sash and Door Co., Phoenix, circa 1946.

Poland, Joseph F. "Subsidence in the U.S. Due to Groundwater Withdrawal." *Journal of Irrigation & Drainage Division,* ASCE, June 1981.

Power, Thomas M. *An Economic Analysis of the Central Arizona Project: U.S. Bureau of Reclamation.* Economics Department, University of Montana, 1978.

———. Testimony on Garrison Diversion Project. University of Montana, March 1977.

———. Economic Analysis of O'Neil Project, Nebraska. University of Montana, May 1978.

———. Oahe Project, Redfield, South Dakota, Benefit-Cost Hearing, University of Montana, March 1977.

———. An Economic Analysis of the Narrows Project. University of Montana, May 1978.

PureCycle Corporation. 1980 Annual Report.

Ralph M. Parsons Company. Letter to author from R.P. Kelly, Vice President, Environmental & Water Engineering, March 25, 1976.

_____. *NAWAPA, North American Water and Power Alliance*, Summary Report for Arizona. November 29, 1965.

_____. *North American Water and Power Alliance, Conceptual Study.* Volume 1, Engineering, December 7, 1974; revised March 1975.

Rappoport, Michael. "SRP Statement before U.S. House Interior and Insular Affairs." Water and Power Resources Subcommittee, January 26, 1982.

Rawlins, Stephen. "Irrigation in a Future Short of Energy." U.S. Salinity Laboratory, Riverside, California, 1980.

Rex, Tom R. "Demographics of the Urban Southwest." *Arizona Business*, Vol. 31, No. 3, Third Quarter, 1984.

Salt River Project. Annual Reports. 1970-82.

_____. Groundwater Recharge Symposium. Phoenix, November 27-28, 1978.

_____. *Major Facts in Brief About SRP*. 1966.

_____. Map of Phoenix and Central Arizona.

_____. *Safety of Dams: SRP Evaluation of CAWCS Candidate Plans.* September 1981.

Scott, Lewis E. "Land Subsidence and Earth Fissuring in Central Arizona." Senior Geological Engineer, Highways Division, Arizona Department of Transportation, presented at ASCE Convention, Portland, Oregon, April 1980.

Sheer, Daniel P., and Kevin Flynn. "Water Supply." *Civil Engineering*, ASCE, June 1983.

Simon, Julian L. "Resources, Population, Environment: An Oversupply of False Bad News." *Science*, Vol. 208, June 27, 1980.

_____. "Are We Losing our Farmland." *The Public Interest*, No. 67, Spring 1982.

_____. "U.S. Farmlands, The False Crisis." The Heritage Foundation "Backgrounder," September 14, 1983.

Simon, Arthur. *Bread for the World*. Paulist Press and Wm. B. Eerdmans Publishing Company, 1975.

Smith, Lawrence P., and Charles W. Stockton. *Reconstructed Stream Flow for the Salt and Verde Rivers from Tree-Ring Data*. Water Resources Bulletin, American Water Resources Association, Vol. 17, No. 6, December 1981.

Smith, Sanford K. "Indian Water Rights: Law and Reality." Presented at ASCE meeting on "Legal, Institutional and Social Aspects of Irrigation and Drainage and Water Resources Planning and Management," Blacksburg, Virginia. July 1978.

Sparks, Felix L. "Synopsis of Major Documents and Events Relating to the Colorado River." Director, Colorado Water Conservation Board, July 1976.

Stephens, Bill. Channel 10 TV documentary interview with head of Municipal Water User Association. On file, circa 1970.

Stockton, C.W. *Long-term Streamflow Records Reconstructed From Tree Rings*. University of Arizona Press, 1975.

Trimble, M. *Arizona, a Panoramic History of a Frontier State*. Doubleday, 1977.

Turner, Kenneth M. "Feed and Forage Crop Projections: Review and Analysis." Office Report, Resource Evaluation Office, California Department of Water Resoruces, May 19, 1977. (Revised October 1977.)

City of Tucson. *The Central Arizona Project. A Staff Report to the Metropolitan Utilities Managment Agency Board and the Mayor and Council of the City of Tucson*. 1974.

U.S. Army Corps of Engineers. *Flood Damage Report, Phoenix Metropolitan Area, December 1978 Flood*. November 1979.

_____. *Historical Highlights of the United States Army Corps of Engineers*. EP 360-1-13, March 1978.

_____. *Phoenix Flood Damage Survey, February 1980*. Los Angeles District. April 1981.

_____. *Nonstructural Measure Investigations, Metropolitan Phoenix Area*. Final Report. December 1980.

U.S. Bureau of Reclamation. *Colorado River Water Quality Improvement Program: Status Report*. January 1974.

_____. *Draft Environmental Impact Statement Regulatory Storage Division, CAP*. April 1983.

_____. *Draft Environmental Statement, Orme Dam and Reservoir, Central Arizona Project, Arizona and New Mexico*. May 1976.

_____. *Environmental Statement, Colorado River Water Quality Improvement Program*. 1976.

_____. *Factbook*. Central Arizona Water Control Study, October 1981.

_____. *Final Environmental Impact Statement, Regulatory Storage Division, CAP*. February, 1984.

_____. *Final Environmental Statement, Central Arizona Project*. 1972.

_____. *Preliminary Engineering Data, Central Arizona Water Control Study*. Prepared by Arizona Project Office, July 1979.

_____. *Safety of Dams Program, Salt River Project, Verde River Unit Addendum*. May 1981.

_____. *Stage III Report, Central Arizona Water Control Study*. Prepared by Arizona Projects Office, April 1983.

_____. *Westwide Study Report on Critical Water Problems Facing the Eleven Western States*. April 1975.

U.S. Comptroller General. *Colorado River Basin Water Problems: How to Reduce Their Impact*. U.S. General Accounting Office, CED-79-11, May 4, 1979.

_____. *Federal Charges for Irrigation Projects Reviewed Do Not Cover Costs*. General Accounting Office, PAD-81-07, March 13, 1981.

_____. *Changes in Federal Water Project Repayment Policies Can Reduce Federal Costs.* GAO, CED-81-77, August 7, 1981.

_____. *Reforming Interest Provisions in Federal Water Laws Could Save Millions.* GAO, CED-82-3, October 22, 1981.

_____. *Reserved Water Rights for Federal and Indian Reservations: A Growing Controversy in Need of Resolution.* GAO, CED-78-176, November 16, 1978.

_____. *Water Project Construction Backlog—A Serious Problem with No Easy Solution.* U.S. General Accounting Office, GAO/RCED-83-49, January 26, 1983.

_____. *Water Supply Should Not Be An Obstacle to Meeting Energy Development Goals.* GAO, CED-80-30, January 24, 1980.

U.S. Congress. Senate. *Congressional Record,* Proceedings and Debates of the 90th Congress, Second Session, Thursday, September 12, 1968. pp. 10648-10673.

_____. House of Representatives. *Dam Safety,* Hearings before a Subcommittee of the Committee on Government Operations. 95th Congress, March 15, 17, and June 30, 1977.

U.S. Department of Agriculture. *1980 Arizona Agricultural Statistics, Historical Summary of County Data, 1965-1980.* Arizona Crop and Livestock Reporting Service, Bulletin S-16, April 1981.

_____. *Economics of Size in Farming.* ERS Report #107 by J. Patrick Mudder, 1967.

_____. *Farmland: Will There Be Enough?* Economic Research Service, ERS-584, May 1975.

_____. *Irrigation with Sewage Effluent.* Proceedings of the Sewage Irrigation Symposium Phoenix, U.S. Water Conservation Laboratory, January 21, 1981.

_____. *Our Land and Water Resources: Current and Prospective Supplies and Uses.* Miscellaneous Publication # 1290, Economic Research Service, May 1974.

U.S. Department of Commerce. *Six-State High Plains Ogallala Aquifer Regional Resources Study.* CDM, Black & Veatch & A.D. Little, Inc. July 1982.

U.S. Department of the Interior, *Central Arizona Project, Arizona, Projects Review.* April 1977.

_____. *Dallas Creek Project. Water Projects Review,* April 1977.

_____. *Dolores Project, Colorado. Water Projects Review,* April 1977.

_____. *Fruitland Mesa Project, CRSP. Water Projects Review,* April 1977.

_____. *Savery-Pot Hook Project, Colorado/Wyoming. Water Projects Review,* April 1977.

_____. *Report on Water for Energy in the Upper Colorado River Basin.* Water for Energy Management Team, July 1974.

U.S. Environmental Protection Agency. *The Mineral Quality Problem in the Colorado River Basin: Summary Report and Appendix A through D.* EPA Regions VII and IX, 1971.

U.S. Fish and Wildlife Service. *The Southern Bald Eagle In Arizona (A Status Report).* Albuquerque, New Mexico, 1976.

U.S. Geological Survey. *Evaporation From the 17 Western States.* Professional Paper 272-D, 1962.

————. *Geohydrology of the Needles Area, Arizona, California and Nevada.* Water Supply Paper #1473, 1959.

————. *Water Demands for Expanding Energy Development.* Circular 703, 1974.

————. *Arizona Water.* Water Supply Paper 1648, 1967.

U.S. Soil Conservation Service. *America's Soil and Water: Condition and Trends.* U.S. Department of Agriculture, December 1980.

U.S. Supreme Court. *Arizona v. California,* 373 U.S. 546, 83 S. Ct. 1468, 10 L.Ed.2d 542, 1963.

————. *Gibbons v. Ogden,* 9 Wheat. 1, 6 L.Ed. 23 (1824).

U.S. Water and Power Resources Services (now Bureau of Reclamation—again). *Acreage Limitation.* Interim Report. March 1980.

U.S. Water Resources Council. *The Nation's Water Resources.* Washington, D.C., 1968.

————. *The Nation's Water Resources 1975-2000, Second National Water Assessment.* December 1978.

University of Arizona. *Water Conservation in the Tucson Active Management Area: An Overview of the Potentials.* Department of Agricultural Economics, April 8, 1983.

University of California. "Salt Management: California's Most Complex Water Quality Problem," Division of Agricultural Sciences, June 1974.

Valley National Bank. "Arizona Progress: Arizona's New Growth Market: Exports." February 1982.

————. *Arizona Statistical Review, 37th Annual Edition.* September 1981.

Vitullo-Martin, Julia. "Ending the Southwest's Water Binge." *Fortune,* February 23, 1981.

Wall Street Journal. "The Issue of the '80s," Review & Outlook. Monday, April 26, 1982.

Water and Power Resources Service. *Memorandum Report on Safety of Dams Program, Salt River Project.* January 1981.

————. *Plan of Study, Central Arizona Water Control Study.* Assisted by U.S. Army Corps of Engineers, January 1980.

————. *Stage II Report, Central Arizona Water Control Study.* Assisted by U.S. Army Corps of Engineers, March 1981.

Water Resources Associates, Inc. *Probable Maximum Flood, Salt and Verde River Basins*; for Arizona Public Service, Co., June 1983.

Watt, James. Secretary of the Interior, quoted in the Water Information News Service. March 22, 1983.

Wilde, K.D., J.E. Keith, and A.D. LeBaron. "Western Economic Development and Water Planning: Bureau of Reclamation."

Closure, *Journal of the Water Resources Planning and Management Division, American Society of Civil Engineers*, March 1982.

Wilson, Mark. "Reclamation Subsidies and Their Present-Day Impact." *Arizona State Law Journal* (1982): 497-537

Woodward, Harry K. "Relative Values of Water." Utah State Water Engineer's Office, December 1, 1974.

Wright, Congressman Jim. *The Coming Water Famine.* Coward McCann Inc. 1966.

Young, R. A. "The Arizona Water Controversy: An Economist's View." Arizona Academy of Science, May 1968.

Young, Robert A., and William Martin. "The Economics of Arizona's Water Problem." *Arizona Review*, Vol. 16, No. 3, March 1967.

Zwick, David, and M. Benstock. *Water Wasteland.* Ralph Nader's Study Group on Water Pollution, Grossman. December 1971.

Index